Y

Reading and Interpreting the Works of

HARPER LEE

Enslow Publishing
101 W. 23rd Street
Suite 240
New York, NY 10011
USA
enslow.com

Lit Crit Guides

Reading and Interpreting the Works of

HARPER LEE

Elizabeth Schmermund

Published in 2017 by Enslow Publishing, LLC
101 W. 23rd Street, Suite 240, New York, NY 10011

Library of Congress Cataloging-in-Publication Data
Names: Schmermund, Elizabeth, author.
Title: Reading and interpreting the works of Harper Lee / Elizabeth Schmermund.
Description: New York, NY : Enslow Publishing, 2017. | Series: Lit crit guides | Includes bibliographical references and index.
Identifiers: LCCN 2016001575 | ISBN 9780766079144 (library bound)
Subjects: LCSH: Lee, Harper--Criticism and interpretation--Juvenile literature.
Classification: LCC PS3562.E353 Z84 2017 | DDC 813/.54--dc23
LC record available at http://lccn.loc.gov/2016001575

Printed in the United States of America

To Our Readers: We have done our best to make sure all website addresses in this book were active and appropriate when we went to press. However, the author and the publisher have no control over and assume no liability for the material available on those websites or on any websites they may link to. Any comments or suggestions can be sent by e-mail to customerservice@enslow.com.

CONTENTS

Harper Lee

AN ENIGMATIC FIGURE

In early 2015, the literary world was set aflame with the announcement of beloved author Harper Lee's second novel, *Go Set a Watchman*. In fact, some people claim to have heard screaming coming from inside the offices of HarperCollins, Harper Lee's publishers, when they made the announcement that a new book was found and would be published. Harper Lee's first novel, *To Kill a Mockingbird,* became an overnight sensation when it was first published in 1960. Her second novel has already caused quite a stir. Some books can change the course of history and become important cultural artifacts for people around the globe. It seems like Harper Lee's novels have done just that.

But Lee's novels—and her fame—have also caused controversy. The announcement of the publication of her second novel in over fifty years led to fiery manifestos and op-eds across major media outlets. Many people criticized those in Harper Lee's closest circles, as well as HarperCollins, for deciding to publish the novel in the first place. They claimed that Lee had not wanted to publish this novel and that she had been coerced into doing so by those eager for monetary gain.

Lee had originally written *Go Set a Watchman* many years ago. In fact, it was the first draft of the book that would later become *To Kill a Mockingbird.* While it shares some famous passages with its later draft, *Go Set a Watchman* is a very different book that takes place in a later time and follows Lee's main character, named Jean Louise Finch, later in life. In 2011, Lee's lawyer was examining the author's safe deposit box when she found the manuscript pages of *Go Set a Watchman*. She read these pages and was so impressed that she contacted Lee and asked if she could send them along to Lee's longtime agent. According to her lawyer and agent, Lee agreed. This discovery changed the course of literary history.

This isn't the only account of the publication of *Go Set a Watchman*, however. Some people claimed that Lee, at the age of eighty-nine, was not well enough to make the decision by herself. Others claimed that Lee's lawyer and agent took advantage of her blindness and memory loss. The state of Alabama, where Lee resides, began an investigation shortly after the publication of the novel was announced, in order to see if Harper Lee was coerced into the agreement. The investigation found that Lee was happy to publish the book and that there was no wrongdoing on the part of her lawyer and agent. But the book has remained controversial. Many authors and literary critics still claim that the book should not have been published in the first place. Some critics have even called for readers to boycott it.

For those not well acquainted with Harper Lee and those closest to her, it's impossible to know the true story behind the publication of *Go Set a Watchman*. Despite the controversy, however, Lee's second book allows readers to reacquaint themselves with old friends: Jean Louise "Scout" Finch and her father, Atticus, among other residents of Maycomb, Alabama. While some familiar characters from *To Kill a Mockingbird* reappear, the world has become a very different place in this second novel. This may be destabilizing for readers and, indeed, some fans of *To Kill a Mockingbird* have derided

Lee's most recent publication. But in *Go Set a Watchman*, Lee continues to do what originally made her a literary star: she brings her characters to life by placing them in complex situations that teach them—and, thus, readers—about the power of compassion in a sometimes cruel world.

A Star Is Born

Harper Lee was born on April 28, 1926, in Monroeville, Alabama. Her birth name was Nelle, although she used her middle name, Harper, as a pen name out of fear that her first name would be mispronounced as "Nellie." Lee's father was a lawyer—some say that he was the inspiration for the character of Atticus Finch in *To Kill a Mockingbird*—and her mother was a homemaker. Her mother's maiden name was Finch. Obviously, Lee drew inspiration for her famous book from her own life.

Early on, Harper Lee was inspired to tell a story about a young girl who experiences racism in her small southern town. In 1949, Lee moved from Monroeville to New York City to find fame as an author. But it didn't work out that well at first. She took a job as a reservation agent at an airline while she wrote short stories and drafts of novels late at night. Then, one Christmas in 1956, she spent the holiday with her friends, Michael and Joy Williams Brown, and their children. She felt sad that she couldn't take a vacation to go home to Alabama and spend Christmas with her family. She also felt frustrated that she didn't have the time to spend on what she was really passionate about—writing.

At the Browns' house on Christmas morning, Lee found an envelope addressed to her under the tree. She opened it and read what was written inside: "You have one year off from your job to write whatever you please. Merry Christmas." She

Lee and her father, Amassa Coleman, or A.C. for short. It is widely believed that Mr. Lee, an editor and lawyer, was the inspiration for the character of Atticus Finch in *To Kill a Mockingbird*.

was confused at first and couldn't believe her friends' generosity. They were offering to pay her expenses for an entire year. She argued with them, telling them what a risk they were taking in believing in her. But they persisted.

Years later, after Harper Lee won the literary world's most prestigious prizes and produced one of the greatest novels ever written, she wrote about how it felt to be given the chance to write *To Kill a Mockingbird*. "A full, fair chance for a new life," she wrote. "Not given me by an act of generosity, but an act of love. *Our faith in you* was really all I had heard them say. I would do my best not to fail them."[1] No one would ever be able to say that she had.

A Powerful, If Quiet, Voice

Before the publication of *Go Set a Watchman,* Lee had only one novel to her name. In addition to *To Kill a Mockingbird*, her first novel, she also published five essays over the course of her literary career: three short reflections on, respectively, love, friendship, and the innocence of children were published in the 1960s, followed by a piece on the history of Alabama in 1983, and, finally, a published letter to Oprah Winfrey about the importance of reading. The words that Lee has published may be few, but they are incredibly powerful. Rarely has one novelist—let alone one novel—had such an effect on American culture.

Immediately upon publication of *To Kill a Mockingbird,* the novel provoked a sensation. It flew off the shelves and eventually would sell more than forty thousand copies worldwide. In the first year of its publication, it was translated into ten languages. Later, it was translated into forty. Less than a year after its publication, Harper Lee won the prestigious Pulitzer

Prize. This was only the beginning of the many awards and honors that Lee and her book would receive.

The power of Lee's voice, and its appeal to readers, comes from the characters she creates in the world of her fiction. Jean Louise Finch, the protagonist of *To Kill a Mockingbird* who is known by her nickname, Scout, tells her story as an adult, looking back at the years between when she was six and nine years old. Her older brother, Jem, grows from age ten to age thirteen over the course of her story. As a young woman, Scout narrates the plot of the novel with the wisdom of an adult, while guarding the innocence and intuition of children. It is this mixture of innocence and wisdom that allows Scout to begin to question and understand the racial inequality that is at the heart of the novel's storyline. While racial segregation and inequality has, tragically, become the norm in many towns, both small and large, across the United States, Scout's

Since its first publication, about forty million copies of *To Kill a Mockingbird* have been sold, and it has been translated into more

childlike wonder allows her to question what adults view as "normal" or "just the way things are."

Lee expressed the faith she puts in children, in particular, in her essay, "When Children Discover America." She writes, "Wordsworth was right when he said that we trail clouds of glory as we come into the world, that we are born with a divine sense of perception. As we grow older, the world closes in on us, and we gradually lose the freshness of viewpoint that we had when we were children."[2]

Lee's works focus on complex issues, but her ability to allow readers to view these issues through the eyes of a child helps us understand them better. Lee's works are about inequality, racial segregation, and oppression. She is a benevolent writer whose sympathy for those who suffer from poverty, racial discrimination, or social stigma is expressed in how she treats each one of her characters. It is through the interactions between characters of various backgrounds, races, and social statuses that we understand the sometimes disheartening ways of the world.

An Outsider's Perspective

The most beloved characters in Harper Lee's works are all outsiders. Many high-society residents of Maycomb, where *To Kill a Mockingbird* and *Go Set a Watchman* are set, misunderstand these characters. Scout is a tomboy who refuses to enter into the conventions of polite, feminine society. Jem is a kind, young boy who attempts to show himself as tougher than he really is. Jem and Scout's best friend, Dill, is a neglected boy who doesn't have a real family to take care of him, although he will do anything to pretend that he is well taken care of. Atticus, Scout and Jem's father, is a single father who lost his wife and his children's mother when Scout was only two years

WILLIAM WORDSWORTH'S "ODE: INTIMATIONS OF IMMORTALITY FROM RECOLLECTIONS OF EARLY CHILDHOOD"

In her 1965 essay "When Children Discover America," Harper Lee writes about the importance of traveling around the United States for American children. This is the way children will discover their country and their world, she says. It is more important for children to learn through their own discoveries, than from having adults give them "absolutely straight answers to everything."[3]

Lee begins her essay with a quote from a poem about childhood experience written by the English poet William Wordsworth. In Wordsworth's "Immortality Ode," as it is known, he expresses his belief that children are aware of a truer existence that gradually fades away as they age. Childhood is closest to that which is true, and we lose this awe-inspiring innocence as we become inducted into this world.

The stanza from which Lee quotes is as follows:

> Our birth is but a sleep and a forgetting:
> The Soul that rises with us, our life's Star,   60
> Hath had elsewhere its setting,
> And cometh from afar:
> Not in entire forgetfulness,
> And not in utter nakedness,
> But trailing clouds of glory do we come   65
> From God, who is our home:
> Heaven lies about us in our infancy!
> Shades of the prison-house begin to close
> Upon the growing Boy,
> But he beholds the light, and whence it flows,   70
> He sees it in his joy;
> The Youth, who daily farther from the east
> Must travel, still is Nature's priest,
> And by the vision splendid
> Is on his way attended;   75
> At length the Man perceives it die away,
> And fade into the light of common day. [4]

In *To Kill a Mockingbird*, Harper Lee shares this belief with Wordsworth—that children are capable of "behold[ing] a light" that only dims as we grow older.

old. He does his best to raise his children morally, but he will not force them to be who they are not, which doesn't always sit well with Maycomb's "polite society." Finally, Calpurnia, the African American woman who works for Atticus and raises Jem and Scout, is a complex figure. She is well educated and a maternal figure in the children's lives. But because of her race, the white residents of Maycomb will not accept her and grow indignant that she plays such a large role in the Finch family's lives.

Boo Radley, perhaps the most enigmatic character in Lee's works, is a true outsider. Afraid of judgment, he never sets foot outside of his home—except to protect Jem and Scout. He is a character who is misunderstood by all except, perhaps, Atticus Finch. By the end of *To Kill a Mockingbird*, Jem and Scout understand that the seemingly strange behavior that makes Boo Radley an outsider in Maycomb is also what makes him the gentlest person they have ever known.

Robert Duvall played the character of Boo Radley, the reclusive but kind neighbor of the Finches, in the film version of *To Kill a Mockingbird*.

15

Perhaps it is the sympathy with which Harper Lee writes about her characters that has made her novels such cherished classics. Lee's most beloved characters share something that many readers may themselves understand—they know the pain it feels to be judged by others or to feel left out or misunderstood. The world Lee's novels reflect is not simpler than our world, and it certainly doesn't treat characters more fairly. However, it is comforting to readers to understand that they are not alone—that others have experienced a pain that they can understand and sympathize with, even if it is in the pages of a book and not in the "real" world.

A Private Life

Monroeville is a small town—less than seven thousand residents inhabit its fifteen square miles (thirty-eight square kilometers)—that sits in southern Alabama. Green pasturelands spread across Monroe County, broken up only by aging plantations that once formed the basis of Alabama's cotton industry on the backs of African American slaves. Today, Monroeville is known as the literary capital of Alabama, and tourists flock to visit the Monroeville Courthouse and the Monroe County Heritage Museum, where theater productions of *To Kill a Mockingbird* are held every year. But when Nelle Harper Lee was born here in 1926, not even the railroad went through the desolate town.

Nelle was one of four children born to Amassa Coleman (A.C.) Lee and Frances Cunningham Finch. Her father was the son of a Civil War veteran and was raised in a strict Methodist household. He became a newspaper editor, lawyer, and school-teacher and was most likely the inspiration for the character of Atticus Finch. Nelle's mother, Frances, came from a wealthy family, received an excellent education, and was a talented piano player. But she suffered from what was most likely undiagnosed manic depression and remained distant from Nelle and her siblings for their entire lives, until her death in 1951. The children adored their father, however, who treated them with the respect normally only reserved for adults. Years later, Nelle would fondly remember how her family stoked her

Harper Lee's hometown of Monroeville, Alabama, shared many similarities with the fictional town of Maycomb from *To Kill a Mockingbird* and *Go Set a Watchman*.

passion for reading—her older siblings read to her, her mother read nightly bedtime stories, and books filled the shelves of the Lee household.

Like Scout, Nelle grew up as a tomboy without the oversight of her mother. She roamed through the backyards of Monroeville in overalls with her best friend, Truman Persons, who played a similar role to Dill in *To Kill a Mockingbird*. Like Dill, Truman was left by his parents in the care of relatives, a nervous boy who made up stories about his life to conceal the hurt caused by his abandonment. When Truman and Nelle were still kids, Nelle's father gave them a treasured gift: an Underwood typewriter. The two had vivid imaginations and brought the typewriter with them everywhere, typing out stories and plays that they would act out in their backyards.

> **nonfiction**
>
> Writing that is based on real-life experience or facts and is not made up.

In the 1930s, Truman was sent to New York City to live with his mother and her new husband. His relationship with Nelle continued, despite their distance. Later, he changed his name to Truman Capote and began, with Nelle's help, to research a nonfiction book that would become *In Cold Blood*, about the murder of the Clutter family in Kansas. This book would make Truman Capote famous.

While at the University of Alabama at Tuscaloosa, Nelle became an editor for the *Rammer Jammer,* the college's satirical publication. On campus, Nelle continued to be known as a tomboy; she rarely wore makeup or dresses and was deemed by some as eccentric. After one semester, Nelle dropped out and moved to New York City. She began to work in a bookstore and as a ticket agent for various airlines. Truman introduced her to Michael Martin Brown and Joy Brown, with whom she

Truman Capote, shown here in 1959, was a close friend of Lee's and the likely inspiration for the character of Dill in *To Kill a Mockingbird*.

would become close friends. Brown was a composer, writer, and lyricist, and when he got a job writing for a Broadway play, he gave money to Nelle so she would have time to work on her novel. She quit her job and began writing immediately.

In 1957, Truman recommended a literary agent to Nelle and soon the manuscript—entitled *Go Set a Watchman*—was sent to various New York publishing houses. Tay Hohoff, an editor at J. B. Lippincott, saw it and was impressed. But she also knew that it needed a lot of work to become ready for publication. She called it "more a series of anecdotes than a fully conceived

> **satire**
>
> A form of humor used to make fun of perceived stupidity. It is especially used to critique politics or social issues.

novel . . . [although] the spark of a true writer flashed in every line."[1] For several years, the editor and author worked together on the manuscript. They became friends and Hohoff provided Nelle with guidance as she revised her manuscript. According to Charles J. Shields, author of *Mockingbird: A Portrait of Harper Lee*, one cold, winter night Lee grew so frustrated with her manuscript that she threw the pages out into the snow. Hohoff convinced the author to go outside immediately and pick up the pages.[2]

Gradually, Hohoff and Lee revised the manuscript of *Go Set a Watchman* into *To Kill a Mockingbird*. The trial of Tom Robinson and Scout, Jem, and Dill's encounter with Boo Radley became the major plot points of the novel—they hadn't even existed in the original manuscript. Hohoff stated, "After a couple of false starts, the story-line, interplay of characters, and fall of emphasis grew clearer, and with each revision—there were many minor changes as the story grew

THE EDITORIAL PROCESS

Books are rarely published in their draft form, as *Go Set a Watchman* was in 2015. Usually, authors work with an editor to revise their manuscript many times before publication. In this way, Harper Lee's experience with *To Kill a Mockingbird* is more typical of an author's experience. Sometimes authors are asked to completely revise a manuscript if an editor likes the idea but does not like its execution. Authors can go through ten or more edits of their manuscript until it is deemed acceptable by their editor.

Even when the manuscript is fully revised, the editorial work is not done. Copyediting is performed on the manuscript, which means an editor reviews it to see if there are any minor grammatical or spelling mistakes. After this, proofreaders normally take one last look at the manuscript. A final proof is sent back to the author for his or her approval. Only after this final step in a long line of revisions is the edited manuscript ready to go out into the world.

in strength and in her own vision of it—the true nature of the novel became evident."[3]

After the publication and success of *To Kill a Mockingbird*, Lee remained close friends with her editor. Hohoff tried to convince Lee to write a second novel, without success. While Lee kept writing, she grew discouraged and overwhelmed by the public's response—and especially the media response—to her book. During Hohoff's years at Lippincott, and for many years after, no one attempted to publish *Go Set a Watchman*,

Alice Lee (left) took care of her younger sister, Harper (right), throughout their lives. They are pictured here celebrating Alice's birthday with Monroe County Judge Dawn Hare.

which was seen as just an earlier version of *To Kill a Mocking-bird.*

According to another Lippincott editor, Edward Burlin-game, Hohoff protected Lee from exploitation because of her success. Burlingame states, "Lippincott's sales department would have published Harper Lee's laundry list . . . But Tay [Hohoff] really guarded Nelle like a junkyard dog. She was not going to allow any commercial pressures or anything else to put stress on her to publish anything that wouldn't make Nelle proud or do justice to her. Anxious as we all were to get another book from Harper Lee, It was a decision we all supported."[4]

Another staunch protector of Lee was her sister, Alice. Alice Lee was Harper's older sister, a well-known Alabama lawyer, and a Methodist church leader. She handled most of her sister's legal affairs and publicity. Requests for interviews often went through Alice first and rarely—if ever—received approval.

The sisters didn't share much in common. Alice was fifteen years older than Harper, and while Harper decided at a young age that she wanted to leave Monroeville for New York City, Alice stayed in her hometown her whole life. Unlike Harper, who is described by those who know her as "spirited," "self-assured," and a force of nature, Alice was more demure and serious. In fact, Harper once called her sister "Atticus in a skirt" who practiced law "sweetly, quietly, and lethally."[5]

Despite their differences, the sisters were close. Although Harper lived in New York for many years, she regularly came home and lived with her sister for weeks or months—just like the older Scout returns home to visit Monroeville. For many of these years, Harper remained out of the spotlight—while her sister ruthlessly guarded her public reputation. Harper briefly came back into the limelight to argue against a Virginia school board's decision to ban *To Kill a Mockingbird* in 1966. But, otherwise, it seemed as if she had disappeared.

In 2007, Harper Lee suffered a stroke and moved back to Monroeville permanently. She stayed largely out of the public eye with the help of those closest to her—at least until the announcement that her second novel would be published in 2015. The following year, on February 19, Lee died at the age of eighty-nine.

A History of Racial and Social Inequity

Harper Lee drew her inspiration for *To Kill a Mockingbird* and *Go Set a Watchman* not only from her own background but also from the difficult history of the southern United States. Lee was raised in Alabama during a time that was fraught with institutionalized racial prejudice and social inequities. In many ways, Lee's works are a direct response to these painful memories of our nation's history—and a call that we cannot forget, both for our past mistakes and for the grassroots activism that allowed for progress.

Setting

Just as the characters make Lee's two novels come alive, so does the setting she chooses. Maycomb, where the Finch family lives, is a character in its own right. As a small town that hasn't changed much in hundreds of years, Maycomb's citizens have been affected by the landscape in which they have been raised.

According to Scout, her father's family originated from Cornwall, England. As a Methodist, her ancestor Simon Finch grew upset at the treatment of Methodists in his home country and gradually made his way to Philadelphia and then to Mobile, Alabama. In the nineteenth century, Simon bought slaves and started a homestead on the banks of the Alabama River. This became known as Finch's Landing. Further generations of Finch men would stay on the homestead and oversee slaves, who were forced to pick cotton in the fields. These slaves had no rights, either on the plantation where they worked or in the larger United States. This was before the Civil War, when African Americans could legally be bought and sold as slaves. The racism inherent in the slave trade is still part of the setting and in the lives of the characters as Scout Finch tells her story, even though slavery was made illegal long before.

The Jim Crow South

Harper Lee's two novels take place in what is often referred to as the Jim Crow South. This name refers to a period of time, from 1890 until 1965, when the Jim Crow laws were in effect throughout many southern states. The Jim Crow laws were local laws in the southern United States that permitted and encouraged racial segregation. They were implemented following the Civil War and the abolishment of slavery in the United States. In effect, they continued the inhumane treatment of African Americans through discriminatory behavior such as segregating public buildings and denying them the right to vote. The motto of the Jim Crow laws was "separate but equal," which meant that black citizens and white citizens would be kept separate but, supposedly, have equal facilities and opportunities. This, however, was not the case. White Americans who lived in the South consistently went to the best public schools and made use of the best restaurants, parks, and housing. Black Americans were only allowed to use inferior facilities; their schools received less funding and, thus, they didn't have the same chance for education.

The harmful effects of slavery and the Jim Crow laws are written into the story of Maycomb. In fact, the Jim Crow laws weren't repealed until 1965, five years after *To Kill a Mockingbird* was published. While *To Kill a Mockingbird* is set in the 1930s, *Go Set a Watchman* takes place nearly twenty years

Unemployed men stand in line for free food during the Depression in the 1920s.

later, as the civil rights movement, an important political movement that fought against the dehumanization of African Americans in the southern United States and forced segregation, began to gain steam.

The Great Depression

Atticus Finch grows up at Finch's Landing. Although his family has an illustrious and wealthy past, their wealth remains in name only. In reality, the Finch family is relatively poor during the course of *To Kill a Mockingbird*. Atticus Finch studies law and works to help pay for his younger brother, John Hale Finch, to go to medical school. After his law studies, Atticus moves to Maycomb, a small but important city twenty miles (32 km) east of Finch's Landing. Maycomb is the government seat of Maycomb County and, thus, it is a large courthouse where Atticus practices law.

Maycomb is a city where everyone knows everyone else. In fact, the Finches are "related by blood or marriage to nearly every family in the town." The town is run-down, and many of its residents are struggling to make ends meet or are living in conditions of poverty. Despite this, Scout states, "it was a time of vague optimism for some of the people: Maycomb County had recently been told that it had nothing to fear but fear itself."[1]

Lee's mention that Maycomb citizens have nothing to fear "but fear itself" provides further insight into the setting of *To Kill a Mockingbird*. This line comes from President Franklin D. Roosevelt's inaugural speech in 1933. This was an important period in the United States because it was at the height of the Great Depression. Following the stock market crash in 1929, the United States experienced one of the greatest and longest-lasting economic depressions ever recorded. This

29

Franklin Delano Roosevelt gives his inaugural speech of 1933, in which he declared, "The only thing we have to fear is fear itself."

Black Friday and the Great Depression

The Great Depression began on October 24, 1929, when the New York stock market began to show signs of stress. Several days later, on October 29, the most devastating stock market crash in history occurred when stock prices rapidly plummeted. Stocks lost most of their worth in that one day, which would become known as Black Tuesday. This signaled the beginning of the United States' greatest economic crisis, which would last ten years.

By 1932, stocks on the New York Stock Exchange were only worth 20 percent of their price before the crash. Nearly half of all American banks had to close their doors.[2] In the process, many Americans lost everything they had worked for their whole lives. Some wealthy families soon found themselves without the money to buy food.

Farmers were hit especially hard during the Great Depression. Families like the Cunninghams, who depended on selling agricultural goods to survive, went bankrupt when prices for these goods fell to a fraction of what they once cost. Almost no one was immune to these devastating economic events, and people grew so desperate that violence often broke out. The Great Depression would come to an end only with increased production because of US involvement in World War II.

period—when Americans saw their fortunes reversed, lost large amounts of money, and many could barely afford to buy food —lasted until 1939.

In Maycomb, the Great Depression affects its residents but occurs in the background of the novel. While many Maycombers, like the Finch family, Mrs. Henry Lafayette Dubose, and Miss Maudie Atkinson, do not seem to be affected by the economic depression, Lee also describes the extreme poverty at the other end of town. Scout and Jem don't understand that they are living through the Depression, but they observe how other families, such as the Cunninghams, live differently than they do, and they ask their father why.

Scout recounts a time when Walter Cunningham needed her father's legal services. Atticus takes the job, but Scout over-hears Cunningham telling her father that he is afraid he won't be able to pay him for his work. Soon, Jem and Scout watch as Walter Cunningham leaves presents such as firewood, hickory nuts, and turnip greens in their backyard. Scout asks her father to explain:

> "Why does he pay you like that?" I asked.
> "Because that's the only way he can pay me. He has no money."
> "Are we poor, Atticus?"
> Atticus nodded. "We are indeed."
> Jem's nose wrinkled. "Are we as poor as the Cunning-hams?"
> "Not exactly. The Cunninghams are country folks, farmers, and the crash hit them hardest."[3]

Maycomb is hit hard by the Great Depression. The Cunningham and the Ewell families, in particular, live in extreme poverty. This is viewed by the characters as part of the social fabric of their town. There are the poor families and

Crowds of people spill out onto the streets of New York City following Black Tuesday, when the stock markets crashed and the country was plunged into an economic depression.

the families who scrape by. The town seems like a magical place to Scout and yet, with the reflection of an adult looking back on her childhood, she understands later that the town is run-down, poor, and steeped in racial and social inequities. As children, Scout and Jem take this for granted. Until the end of *To Kill a Mockingbird*, they believe this is the way that life is and must be. Only later do they start to understand that complacency is at fault in Maycomb County. People need to stand up for what they believe in, as Atticus Finch does in *To Kill a Mockingbird*, no matter what the cost.

INNOCENCE LOST AND FOUND: MAJOR THEMES

W hen *To Kill a Mockingbird* grew enormously successful in the years following its publication, it became very difficult for Harper Lee to manage the barrage of requests for interviews. She soon stopped granting any interviews and remained largely silent about her novels after that. The last major interview Lee gave was in 1964 to Roy Newquist. In response to a question about her newfound fame, Lee answered:

> It was like being hit over the head and knocked cold. You see, I never expected any sort of success with *Mockingbird*. I didn't expect the book to sell in the first place. I was hoping for a quick and merciful death at the hands of reviewers, but at the same time I sort of hoped that maybe someone would like it enough to give me encouragement . . . I hoped for a little, as I said, but I got rather a whole lot, and in some ways this was just about as frightening as the quick, merciful death I'd expected.[1]

In a 2015 interview Lee gave for the release of *Go Set a Watchman*, she made the reporter promise not to mention her first book. Because of Lee's reluctance to speak about the motivations for her writing, it is hard to know why she wrote *To Kill a Mockingbird*. Lee never spoke about her personal beliefs and the racial segregation she saw as a white girl growing up in Alabama.

Lee's intense privacy, and the fact that she never wrote or published another book after *To Kill a Mockingbird*—with the exception, of course, of *Go Set a Watchman*, which is considered by many critics to be an earlier draft of her famous novel and not a stand-alone work of fiction—has led many people to speculate about the provenance of the novel. Some have even proposed that Harper Lee's good friend, Truman Capote, a literary giant in his own right, wrote *To Kill a Mockingbird*. However, this rumor is unfounded. A recently discovered letter written by Truman Capote, in which he describes reading Lee's manuscript a year before it was published, proves this rumor false.

provenance

The beginning of something; in literary terms, how a piece of writing originally came about.

The dearth of information from Lee means that critics and students must analyze her published words, as well as their historical context, without relying on outside information. This is called close literary analysis, when readers pay close attention to the words of a literary text in order to understand such things as the author's intent and the use of imagery, metaphors, symbolism, and other literary techniques.

Literary themes are a form of literary device that express—sometimes clearly, sometimes in a more complex way—the overall meaning of a work of fiction. By exploring the literary themes present in *To Kill a Mockingbird* and *Go Set a Watchman*, we can piece together the meaning—or, more accurately, the multiple meanings—of a literary work.

Lee expresses complex ideas through the themes she explores in both of her works, including innocence, racial inequality, poverty, gender roles and societal expectations, and compassion.

Harper Lee visited Monroeville in 1961, not long after the publication of *To Kill a Mockingbird*.

Children's Innocence

Scout narrates both novels as an adult, exploring a specific three-year period of time in *To Kill a Mockingbird* and her general childhood mixed with her current relationships with her family in *Go Set a Watchman*. Because the plots of both novels are so rooted in Scout's childhood, she is able to show her world in a different light than adults are used to seeing.

To Kill a Mockingbird begins with an epigraph by Charles Lamb, an English writer best known for his children's books: "Lawyers, I suppose, were children once." This quote introduces, even before the beginning of the novel, the obvious but often overlooked fact that everyone was once a child—even, perhaps, the wiliest lawyers—who looked at the world with innocence, unaware of the harm people could cause one another.

The novel itself begins with the plot's ending: Jem's injury after Bob Ewell attacks him and Scout because of Atticus's support of Tom Robinson. Scout recounts, "When enough years had gone by to enable us to look back on them, we sometimes discussed the events leading to his accident. I maintain that the Ewells started it all, but Jem, who was four years my senior, said it started long before that."[2]

Here, Harper Lee sets up the important theme of childhood and the divide between understanding the events that shape our lives as children and then as adults. Scout states that she and Jem hadn't truly been able to reflect on the events

symbolism
The use of symbols, or a thing that represents something else, to convey a theme or ideas.

metaphor
A literary device used to compare something to an unrelated thing for literary effect.

that shaped their lives until they were older. They hadn't understood their significance then.

That doesn't mean that Scout and Jem totally lack understanding—it just means that they don't see the consequences of major events in their lives as an adult, like their father, Atticus, would. In fact, Harper Lee suggests throughout the novel that the innocence of childhood allows us to look at the world in a new light—and maybe, it is just this that will make the world a better place.

That's not to say that Jem and Scout grow up protected from the often-cruel adult world. Jem and Scout are not

In a dramatic scene from the film, Jem is attacked by Bob Ewell, causing his arm to be broken.

protected from real life by Atticus the way other Maycomb children are protected by their families. Atticus advises his brother, Jack, not to underestimate children. He says, "When a child asks you something, answer him, for goodness' sake. But don't make a production of it. Children are children, but they can spot an evasion quicker than adults, and evasion simply muddles 'em."[3]

For Atticus, children see the world differently than adults—but that doesn't mean that they are incapable of understanding what is going on around them.

Racial Inequality

Racial inequality is a strong force in Maycomb. When towns-people discover that Atticus is taking on Tom Robinson's defense, children mock Scout and Jem at school, armed with words they have overheard from their parents' conversations. Scout hears what her neighbors really think about the African American residents of Maycomb during a ladies' luncheon that Aunt Alexandra hosts at the Finch residence. Mrs. Merriweather states, "Gertrude, I tell you there's nothing more distracting than a sulky darky. Their mouths go down to here. Just ruins your day to have one of 'em in the kitchen. You know what I said to my Sophy, Gertrude? I said, 'Sophy,' I said, 'you simply are not being a Christian today. Jesus Christ never went around grumbling and complaining,' and you know it did her good."[4]

Mrs. Merriweather uses racist, derogatory terms to refer to African Americans and a condescending tone. She does not see—or pretends not to see—that Tom Robinson's conviction could have been upsetting to his family and friends—and symbolic of a larger problem of racial injustice. Miss Maudie soon puts Mrs. Merriweather in her place. Scout reflects soon after this, "Well, neither [Mrs. Merriweather nor me] was the Mayor of Birmingham, but I wished I was the Governor of Alabama for one day: I'd let Tom Robinson go so quick the Missionary Society wouldn't have time to catch its breath."[5] Scout is eager, like her father, for justice to prevail, but she can't yet totally understand the racism that undergirds the unjust trial of Tom Robinson. She understands that Tom Robinson is an innocent man, but can't comprehend the complexity of the situation that finds him guilty—just because of the color of his skin.

Later on, when Atticus rushes in and tells Miss Maudie, Aunt Alexandra, and Scout that Tom Robinson has just been shot and killed for allegedly trying to escape from prison, Miss Maudie makes an impassioned speech. "The handful of people in this town [who trust Atticus to do the right thing]," she says, ". . .say that fair play is not marked White Only; the handful of people who say a fair trial is for everybody, not just us; the handful of people with enough humility to think, when they look at a Negro, there but for the Lord's kindness am I."[6]

Harper Lee has noted in one of her rare interviews that she "tried to give a sense of proportion to life in the South, that there isn't a lynching before every breakfast. I think that Southerners react with the same kind of horror as other people do about the injustice in their land."[7] Part of Lee's motivation for writing *To Kill a Mockingbird* was to dispel the belief—especially among people from the northern United States—that southerners didn't care about racial injustice in the Jim Crow South. She wanted to show readers that there were southerners who cared and fought for what was right, including Atticus Finch.

Atticus's advocacy for racial justice in *To Kill a Mockingbird* becomes problematic in *Go Set a Watchman*. In this second novel, set twenty years later, racial prejudice continues to thwart justice for African Americans in Maycomb and elsewhere in the United States. However, Atticus Finch no longer appears as the hero of the story—in fact, Atticus's complacency in the face of racial injustice threatens his relationship with his daughter.

Poverty

The divisions in Maycomb don't exist only between white and black residents, but also between poor and wealthier residents. The Cunninghams and Conninghams are poorer families who live on the border of Maycomb in an area called Old Sarum. The Cunninghams (and Conninghams) live here, as well as the Ewells, and many African American residents of Maycomb, including Tom Robinson and his family. This is the poorest part of town, located on sparse farmland. Children in the schoolyard whisper about their poorer counterparts who come from this region. Later, the extreme poverty of the Ewells, in particular, will play into the trial of Tom Robinson. Scout's—and other Maycomb residents'—opinion of these people is largely based on their lower social class.

Henry, Scout's childhood friend and boyfriend in *Go Set a Watchman*, explains at the end of the book what it is like to grow up poor in Maycomb. When Scout yells at Henry for being part of the citizens' councils with Atticus, he says, "I'm part of Maycomb County's trash, but I'm part of Maycomb County. I'm a coward, I'm a little man, I'm not worth killing, but this is my home . . . I am trying to make you see, my darling, that you are permitted a sweet luxury I'm not. You can shout to high heaven, I cannot. How can I be of any use to a town if it's against me?"[8]

Bob Ewell stands with Atticus Finch at the trial of Tom Robinson.

Henry explains to Scout that she is privileged because she comes from a well-known and well-respected family name. She has the liberty to speak her mind about racial intolerance, while he does not. In order to be respected despite his poor upbringing in Maycomb, he must fit in with the rest of Maycomb. He calls himself part of Maycomb's "trash." In fact, Aunt Alexandra has already vocalized this belief to Scout. She reminds Scout several times throughout the novel that Henry would not be an appropriate husband for her because, although he is now a successful lawyer working with Atticus, he was born poor to a single mother. He doesn't have the social status that Scout does.

Scout does not understand her privilege at first. In fact, she is so angry at her father that she barely hears what Henry is telling her. But what he tells her is apt: Scout is given privilege to act against the grain in a way that other people are not. Different citizens in Maycomb—whether they are white, black, rich, or poor—must act according to their status. If they do not, they will most likely be punished or put back in place, unless they come from the more respected and educated levels of society, where they have a greater chance to rebel against Maycomb's expectations of them.

Gender Roles and Societal Expectations

Henry's speech allows readers to understand why Scout is allowed to rebel against societal norms in other ways in Maycomb's polite society. Although she is often corrected by her Aunt Alexandra, she does not suffer from her decision, as a young girl, to wear pants instead of a dress. In *Go Set a Watchman*, Scout rebels against Maycomb's expectation that she should marry a suitable partner, settle down, and have children. It is expected that she should enter into the polite society of Maycomb, dress delicately, and host ladies' luncheons as her Aunt Alexandra does so proudly.

But Scout does not want this life for herself. She states explicitly that this is the reason why she has had to leave Maycomb. She doesn't fit into the expectations of what a Finch daughter should be. She wants to continue her career and live life as she chooses to, without being forced to fulfill a particular gender role.

In *To Kill a Mockingbird*, Scout states, "Aunt Alexandra was fanatical on the subject of my attire. I could not possibly hope to be a lady if I wore breeches; when I said I could do nothing in a dress, she said I wasn't supposed to be doing things that required pants. Aunt Alexandra's vision of my deportment involved playing with small stoves, tea sets, and wearing the Add-A-Pearl necklace she gave me when I was born; furthermore, I should be a ray of sunshine in my father's lonely life."[9]

Scout's "unfeminine" behavior is often blamed on the fact that she is raised by a single father after the death of her

GENDER AND GENDER ROLES

Gender refers to the societal roles that men and women are expected to follow. Gender should not be conflated with biological sex and, in some societies, there are more genders than just male and female.

Gender roles often change depending on the culture and historical time period in which they are set. In Alabama during the 1930s, when Scout is a girl, girls were expected to be seen and not heard, to wear dresses, and to play with other girls instead of boys. Girls were also expected not to play outside or to get dirty. These are all societal rules that Scout flouts—in the process making her Aunt Alexandra very mad.

mother when she is two years old. In fact, Aunt Alexandra suggests that this is why she stays with Atticus—not just to provide him with some help while he works on an important court case, but also to add a little womanly direction in Scout's life.

In *To Kill a Mockingbird,* Jem threatens his younger sister several times that, if she becomes more like a girl, he won't want to play with her anymore. Scout says, "Jem told me I was being a girl, that girls always imagined things, that's why other people hated them so, and if I started behaving like one I could just go off and find some to play with."[10] Scout idolizes her older brother, and she has little use for the girls in her class. As we read about Scout's high school years in *Go Set a Watchman,* we find out that she continued to hang out with Jem and other male friends, but rarely the girls in her school.

Scout is not the only one who defies societal expectations in Maycomb. Perhaps the figure who is the biggest outsider to Maycomb society is Arthur Radley. Known as Boo, the Finch's neighbor fascinates Scout and Jem because he never leaves his house. Many rumors circulate about him, from his being a criminal to his being a ghost. Jem gives a description of Boo: "Boo was about six-and-a-half feet tall, judging from his tracks; he dined on raw squirrels and any cats he could catch, that's why his hands were bloodstained—if you ate an animal raw, you could never wash the blood off. There was a long jagged scar that ran across his face; what teeth he had were yellow and rotten; his eyes popped, and he drooled most of the time."[11] Of course, Jem has never seen him and invents this character to scare Dill and Scout—as well as to make himself seem more courageous and mature. Miss Stephanie Crawford, a neighbor whose favorite pastime is gossiping, tells Jem that, when scrapbooking, he drove a pair of scissors into his father's

Scout finally comes face-to-face with Boo Radley after he saves her and Jem from Bob Ewell.

legs years ago. Instead of being put in an asylum, the sheriff locked Boo in the courthouse basement for years, until he was finally transferred to his home, which he never left.

The children are fascinated by Boo Radley and play games trying to get him to come out of the house. Jem tries to prove he is the most courageous by running up to the Radley house and sneaking inside. The kids then play games on their front lawn, pretending to be Boo and his family.

But Scout and Jem's fears are proved false when Bob Ewell attacks them on the way home from the school pageant. Boo Radley saves them from Ewell's vicious attack and accompanies the children back to their home. Boo doesn't speak and is obviously uncomfortable in the presence of other people. But, by this time, Scout has understood that Boo is not an evil—or even weird—person, but rather a shy and gentle person who has difficulty acting in the way that Maycomb's society expects him to act. Scout says:

> I was beginning to learn his body English. His hand tightened on mine and he indicated that he wanted to leave.
>
> I led him to the front porch, where his uneasy steps halted. He was still holding my hand and he gave no sign of letting me go.
>
> "Will you take me home?"
>
> He almost whispered it, in the voice of a child afraid of the dark.[12]

At the end of *To Kill a Mockingbird*, Scout feels a sense of complicity with Boo. It is because she is a child that Scout is able to understand Boo without the judgment of an adult. But it is also because Scout herself experiences what it is like to live as an outsider in Maycomb—even if she is an outsider who is granted a certain amount of leniency to transgress, as Henry states.

Tolerance and Compassion

It is through her experience of Tom Robinson's trial and her encounter with Boo Radley that Scout learns the importance of tolerance and compassion. In *To Kill a Mockingbird* Scout is too young to completely understand why Tom Robinson does not receive a fair trial; as she grows she develops a fierce sense of justice. When she returns to Maycomb in *Go Set a Watchman*, Scout comes back with a strong sense of social justice. She believes strongly in what is right and is prepared to stand up for equality—even if she must break her relationship with her father.

The title of *Go Set a Watchman* refers to Scout's developing sense of morality. It comes from the Book of Isaiah in the Bible: "For thus hath the Lord said unto me, Go, set a watchman, let him declare what he seeth."[13] In the Book of Isaiah, the prophet warns about the fall of the great city of Babylon because of the sins of the Babylonians. Isaiah is the "watchman" who must declare what he sees as morally wrong. Everyone has a sense of right and wrong; in this quote from the Bible, those who observe wrongdoing must speak out against it.

Wayne Flynt, a close friend of Harper Lee and a Baptist minister, has said that Lee was raised in a Christian family and was influenced by the King James Bible in particular. He says, "Nelle [Harper Lee] probably likened Monroeville to Babylon . . . The Babylon of immoral voices, the hypocrisy. Somebody needs to be set as the watchman to identify what we need to do to get out of the mess."[14] *Go Set a Watchman* was most likely the original title for *To Kill a Mockingbird* but was considered too obscure. In *To Kill a Mockingbird*, the watchman is Atticus, who takes on the defense of Tom Robinson because he could not live with himself if an innocent man was condemned only because of the color of his skin. However, *Go Set a Watchman* complicates Atticus Finch. In fact, in this second novel Atticus is no longer a watchman of what is right. It is now up to Scout to stand up for what she believes in, even if it means going against her adored father.

Toward the end of the novel, Uncle Jack explains this to Scout, who doesn't yet understand that she must rebel against her father in order to take a stand for her own beliefs. He says:

> Every man's island, Jean Louise, every man's watchman, is his conscience. There is no such thing as a collective conscious . . . now you, Miss, born with your own conscience, somewhere along the line fastening it like a barnacle onto your father's. As you grew up, when you were grown, totally unknown to yourself, you confused your father with God. You never saw him as a man with a man's heart, and a man's failings . . . You had to kill yourself, or he had to kill you to get you functioning as a separate entity.[15]

Atticus Finch fails in Harper Lee's second novel as a force of justice. He grows older and loses his moral compass in the face of change. It is oftentimes hard for people who are so used to living in a particular way to accept change in their lives. Scout, as a young woman, does not have this same reticence for change. In this sense, *Go Set a Watchman* is a story about growing up and becoming one's own person. For Scout this means that she must not only doggedly pursue her own beliefs, against both racial discrimination and conformity, but that she must also learn to be compassionate. As Uncle Jack says:

You're color blind, Jean Louise. . .You always have been, you always will be. The only differences you see between one human and another are differences in looks and intelligence and character and the like. You've never been prodded to look at people as a race, and now that race is the burning issue of the day, you're still unable to think racially. You see only people.[16]

To Kill a Mockingbird

Harper Lee has long insisted that *To Kill a Mockingbird* is not autobiographical and, thus, not based on her own life. But there are some similarities that are hard to ignore, including the Finch family name, the fact that Atticus shared a profession—and, seemingly, a temperament—with Harper's own father, and the influence of Lee's hometown of Monroeville on the fictitious Maycomb.

Shortly after Amasa Coleman Lee, Harper's father, passed the Alabama bar exam, he worked on a controversial case in which two black men were accused of murdering a white man. Amasa Lee lost the case and the two black men—a father and son—were hanged. Supposedly, he was so disgusted with the unfair trial and the unjust execution of these two men that he gave up criminal law.

When Harper Lee was ten years old—about the same age as Scout Finch—a white woman near Monroeville falsely accused a black man of rape. Her father's newspaper covered the trial. Some people also state that this provided inspiration for the young Lee's later book. Her father's careers as a lawyer and a newspaper publisher both provided ample examples of the unjust trials and executions of African Americans at the time.

These trials profoundly affected Lee, as they affected many people who lived through them. Northerners and southerners were often divided over these trials, either arguing that the

Lee sits in the Monroeville courthouse, which was the model for her courthouse scenes in *To Kill a Mockingbird*.

men had been brought to justice or that the racial prejudice made legal justice impossible under the Jim Crow South. History would prove that the latter was true.

In a 1961 interview that Lee granted before she stopped speaking with the media, she stood in the Monroeville Courthouse and had her picture taken. She spoke of the trial depicted in *To Kill a Mockingbird*:

> The trial was a composite of all the trials in the world— some in the South. But the courthouse was this one. My father was a lawyer, so I grew up in this room and mostly watched him from here. My father is one of the few men I've known with genuine humility, and it lends him a natural dignity. He has absolutely no ego drive, and so he was one of the most beloved men in this part of the state.[1]

This was how the book started, Lee said. It began as a "love story" to her father—and perhaps to her town.[2] She mentioned that in writing *To Kill a Mockingbird*, she also sought to reconcile her life in the North versus her childhood in the South. She wanted people in New York City to know that many people in the South wanted to support the civil rights movement—although they perhaps had different perspectives on how to go about doing it. In one of her last interviews, Lee repeated her belief in the civil rights movement and her plea to her fellow southerners to understand the importance of racial equality. When asked by a reporter what she thought about the "freedom riders" (civil rights activists who rode on buses in the South in order to protest segregation), she answered:

> I don't think much of this business of getting on buses and flaunting state laws does much of anything. Except getting a lot of publicity and violence. I think Reverend King and the NAACP [National Association for the

Advancement of Colored People] are going about it exactly the right way. The people in the South may not like it but they respect it . . . [*To Kill a Mockingbird*] is not an indictment [against any group] so much as a plea for something, a reminder to people at home.[3]

Lee could never have imagined that this "reminder to people at home," would become a beloved classic to people all around the world—even to those who never lived in the South or later generations who could not understand the racial injustice that occurred under Jim Crow.

Structure

To Kill a Mockingbird is divided into two parts and thirty chapters. The first part of the book follows Jem, Scout, and Dill around on their adventures over a period of two years. The novel starts in a flashback and then returns to the story of the three children's adventures in front of the Radley house. The seasons move quickly—Dill leaves at the summer's end and then comes back again. Jem grows older, joins football at his new school, and distances himself from his younger sister.

> **narrative structure**
>
> The way in which the content of a story is organized and presented to the reader.

The second part of the story focuses less on Boo Radley—until, of course, he returns as a hero at the end of the novel—and more on Tom Robinson's trial and the consequences of this court case.

> **first-person narration**
>
> When one person narrates the story using the first-person "I."

This part focuses on a much shorter period of time—a period of six months or so from the beginning of the summer, when Dill sneaks back to Maycomb—until early fall, when Jem and

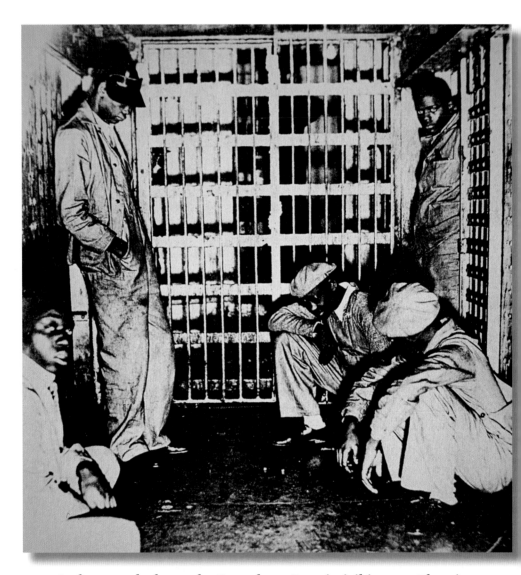

A photograph shows the Scottsboro Boys in jail in 1931. The nine teens were wrongly accused of raping two white women.

The Scottsboro Boys Case

Many people point to the famous Scottsboro case as an influence in the creation of *To Kill a Mockingbird*. Known as the Scottsboro Boys, nine African American teenagers were accused of raping two white women in 1931. Supposedly, the attack occurred on a train traveling between Alabama and Tennessee. The case was tried in Scottsboro, Alabama, close to where the incident was reported, first by a group of young white men and then by the women themselves.

This case showed the miscarriage of justice that occurred during many trials against African Americans, and especially African American men. The selected jury was made of white men and women, the defendants were not granted acceptable legal representation, and the case itself was rushed. Within a month, eight of the nine teenagers had been convicted and sentenced to death. Throughout the case, lynch mobs threatened the lives of the young men.

Following evidence that the men were innocent, based on a letter one of the women wrote to a friend denying that she was raped, the United States Supreme Court decided to hear the case. The Supreme Court decided that the trial had been unfair because the men were denied proper legal representation, which necessitated a retrial. During a retrial, the young woman admitted that she had lied and that she had not been raped. The all-white jury still found the defendants guilty, and the judge threw out the case. Another retrial was scheduled. However, the judge appointed for this new trial was clearly biased against the black men. Another guilty verdict—and punishment by execution—was handed down and the case was sent back to the US Supreme Court, which ruled that African Americans should be represented on juries. These retrials continued for some time. Eventually, charges were dropped against the men, but most of them served jail time. In 2013, Alabama's parole board finally granted posthumous pardons to several of the Scottsboro Boys who hadn't lived to see the guilty verdict against them overturned.

Scout are attacked by Bob Ewell on the way home from their school pageant.

Narration and Plot

Scout narrates the events of the novel in close first person. But she is no longer a child when she recounts these events that shaped her life. As the narrator, the adult Scout looks back at a period of three years during her childhood that changed the course of her life.

The novel begins with these paragraphs:

> When he was nearly thirteen, my brother Jem got his arm badly broken at the elbow. When it healed, and Jem's fears of never being able to play football were assuaged, he was seldom self-conscious about his injury. His left arm was somewhat shorter than his right; when he stood or walked, the back of his hand was at right angles to his body, his thumb parallel to his thigh. He couldn't have cared less, so long as he could pass and punt.
>
> When enough years had gone by to enable us to look back on them, we sometimes discussed the events leading to his accident. I maintain that the Ewells started it all, but Jem, who was four years my senior, said it started long before that. He said it began the summer Dill came to us, when Dill first gave us the idea of making Boo Radley come out.[4]

The first lines set up the rest of the novel. Readers understand, in just these two paragraphs, that an adult is looking back over a period of time in her childhood when her brother was about to turn thirteen. Readers also understand that the event that led to Jem's broken arm is incredibly important to

Lee poses with Mary Badham, the young actress who portrayed Scout in the film version of *To Kill a Mockingbird*.

the story—and that it is a somewhat complicated matter that will be recounted throughout the course of the book.

James McBride, author of the well-known memoir *The Color of Water*, has said that the first paragraph is one of his favorites in the whole novel. He states:

> This paragraph sets up the whole book . . . It sets up the whole story. By speaking to the specific, the story of how her brother broke his arm, she speaks to the general problem of four hundred years of racism, slavery, socio-economic classism, problems between classes, problems between people who have, people who don't, the courage of the working class, the isolation of the South, the identity crises of a young girl, and the coming out of a neighborhood recluse. All that in the story of her brother, who, when he was nearly thirteen, broke his arm.[5]

Scout's narration is deceivingly simple. It seems like it will be a child's story—a simple recounting of her older brother's accident and the events that led up to it. However, as McBride states, this is not the case at all. This deceptively simple beginning alludes to a whole history of racial injustice, the consequences of poverty, and the pains of growing up—and understanding that the world is not what you once imagined it to be.

Jem and Scout are outsiders who grow up under the care of their single father, Atticus, after the death of their mother when they are very young. They grow up in Monroeville, a small town in Alabama, at the height of the Great Depression during the mid-1930s. Jem and Scout's closest friend is Dill, a strange boy who comes back to Maycomb every summer to stay with his aunt. Dill and Scout have a special connection—

Scout looks up to Dill, who is older than she is, and Dill states that they will one day marry.

The kids are obsessed with their next-door neighbor, Arthur (Boo) Radley, who lived with his parents until they died and now lives in the care of his brother. He never leaves the house and rumors spread among the children of Maycomb as to why he isolates himself. During this time, Jem and Scout find little presents for them tucked into a hole in a tree in the Radleys' yard. Jem tries to sneak into the Radley house one night and almost gets shot by Nathan Radley, Boo's older brother. After a while, Nathan Radley plugs up the knothole of the tree on his property. Scout believes that it is Boo who is placing presents in the tree for her, although she doesn't tell anyone. One day, Scout watches as a neighbor's house catches on fire. Without knowing it, someone places a blanket on her shoulders to protect her from the cold. Could this be Boo Radley, too?

Soon, rumors about a new trial that Atticus has taken on spread around town. Scout and Jem are teased in class because their father is defending a black man named Tom Robinson against the accusation of raping a white woman named Mayella Ewell. Scout is largely unaware of the racism that runs rampant in Maycomb and can't grasp the full meaning of the nasty insults she hears adults and kids speaking about her father and Tom Robinson.

On the day of the trial, Jem, Scout, and Dill sneak into the courthouse. They sit in the "colored balcony" with the friends of their beloved African American housekeeper, Calpurnia. During the trial it becomes obvious to the children that Tom Robinson is innocent and that Bob Ewell, Mayella's father, fabricated the story to hide his own abuse of the children. When the guilty verdict is handed back to the judge by the

Bob Ewell takes the witness stand and falsely accuses Tom Robinson, a black man, of raping his daughter.

all-white jury, the children are disgusted, frustrated, and even despondent. Several weeks later, during a ladies' luncheon with her Aunt Alexandra, Scout learns that Tom Robinson has been killed trying to escape from the prison in which he was held.

At the beginning of fall, after Dill has left to return home to Mississippi, Jem and Scout are walking back home from a school pageant when they are attacked by Bob Ewell. Jem's arm is broken and he is badly injured. The attack on them is stopped by a mysterious figure, who turns out to be Boo Radley. He protects the children from Ewell, killing him in the attack, and carries Jem back home. Scout understands that Boo Radley is not an evil figure, but a misunderstood man who has looked out for her and her brother the only way he knows how.

At the end of the novel, it seems as if Scout has grown into the understanding that her father, Atticus, attempted to teach her through his own actions—all people are human and need to be treated with compassion and equality. This powerful revelation remains neatly contained in this book—but is questioned and complicated in *Go Set a Watchman*.

Literary Techniques

As Lee introduces the town of Maycomb to readers, she writes:

> Maycomb was an old town, but it was a tired old town when I first knew it. In rainy weather the streets turned to red slop; grass grew on the sidewalks, the courthouse sagged in the square. Somehow it was hotter then: a black dog suffered on a summer's day; bony mules hitched to Hoover carts flicked flies in the sweltering shade of the live oaks on the square. Men's stiff collars wilted by nine in the morning. Ladies bathed before noon, after their three-o'clock naps, and by nightfall

were like soft teacakes with frostings of sweat and sweet talcum.

Author Wally Lamb chose this paragraph as an example of the literary mastery of *To Kill a Mockingbird*. He states, "It is a one-paragraph course on writing, those tactile sensations, that's real writing. That's literature."[6]

Indeed, Lee's masterful use of sensory details and imagery are what makes the town of Maycomb come alive to readers. Instead of just expressing the heat of Maycomb by referring to temperatures, she provides detailed imagery ("men's stiff collars wilted by nine in the morning," and ladies who became "like soft teacakes with frostings of sweat and sweet talcum" by nightfall).

Lee also uses foreshadowing to create a sense of tension in the plot of *To Kill a Mockingbird*. While Boo Radley seems to have no connection with the trial and subsequent events in the lives of the Finch children, readers understand belatedly that Boo's protection is foreshadowed earlier in the novel. Although it is never stated, Scout hints that Boo Radley put gifts into the hollow of the tree—signifying his distant but friendly feelings for the children. Scout believes—although it remains largely unstated—that Boo was the one who placed a blanket over her shoulders to protect her from the cold the night of the fire. These events seem to have little significance until the last scenes of the novel.

Tom Robinson's trial initially seems like a plot twist. Up until this point, race does not play a leading role in the plot of the novel. This is because Scout remains largely ignorant of the larger racial and social inequities in Maycomb. It is only the adult narrator Scout who is able to comprehend—and express—the importance of the events that took place over this period of time.

Symbolism

Harper Lee also uses symbolism to express the themes of the book. In particular, the animals in the book represent larger ideas—such as innocence and the dangers of racial prejudice. The mockingbird is the most obvious symbol in the book. After Uncle Jack gives Jem and Scout two air rifles, Atticus refuses to teach them how to shoot.

imagery

The author's use of vivid language and description to paint a visual picture for his or her readers.

sensory details

Writing that engages at least one of the reader's five senses: sight, sound, taste, touch, and smell.

Instead, he gives them this advice: "I'd rather you shot at tin cans in the back yard, but I know you'll go after birds. Shoot all the bluejays you want, if you can hit 'em, but remember it's a sin to kill a mockingbird."[7]

Scout reflects: "That was the only time I ever heard Atticus say it was a sin to do something, and I asked Miss Maudie about it.

'Your father's right,' she said. 'Mockingbirds don't do one thing but make music for us to enjoy. They don't eat up people's gardens, don't nest in corncribs, they don't do one thing but sing their hearts out for us. That's why it's a sin to kill a mockingbird.'"[8]

The mockingbird symbolizes innocence—an innocence that cannot, and must not, be destroyed. This innocence can be applied both to the characters of Tom Robinson

plot twist

An unexpected event that changes the course of the plot.

The mockingbird is a symbol of innocence in Lee's novel.

and to Boo Radley. But, while Tom Robinson is killed despite his innocence, Boo Radley's innocence is preserved.

Another animal that serves as a symbol in the book is Tim Johnson, a beloved dog who is referred to as "the pet of Maycomb." Scout and Jem spot Tim Johnson wandering down the street, twitching and foaming at the mouth. This is a sign of rabies, and the children alert Calpurnia and then their father.

The only thing that Atticus can do is shoot the dog in order to protect the lives of the neighbors. Atticus hates guns—although the children never find out why—and hasn't used a gun in many years. But he takes the rifle and shoots Tim Johnson with an expert shot—surprising Scout at his comfort with the gun. Miss Maudie explains to them that his name as a kid was "One-Shot" and that he was the "deadest shot in Maycomb county in his time."[9]

Miss Maudie says, "The very idea, didn't you know his nickname was Ol' One-Shot when he was a boy? Why, down at the Landing when he was coming up, if he shot fifteen times and hit fourteen doves he'd complain about wasting ammunition."[10]

Scout wonders aloud why Atticus has never mentioned this and never goes hunting anymore. Miss Maudie responds:

> If your father's anything, he's civilized in his heart. Marksmanship's a gift of God, a talent—oh, you have to practice to make it perfect, but shootin's different from playing the piano or the like. I think maybe he put his gun down when he realized that God had given him an unfair advantage over most living things. I guess he decided he wouldn't shoot till he had to, and he had to today.[11]

This moment symbolizes the destruction of innocence, solidifies Atticus's status of hero to the children, and foreshadows the death of Tom Robinson by gunshot. Of course, Tom Robinson is not being compared to the dog. However, the dog is an innocent whose life must be sacrificed. Tom Robinson is innocent of his crime, but his life is sacrificed by an all-white jury. But perhaps his death is what awakens Scout and the other children to the dangers of racial inequality—and changes Maycomb for the better.

Style

An author's literary style refers to the language used throughout a literary work to communicate the story and its main themes. Harper Lee's story is simple and concise. She does not spend a lot of time on unnecessary descriptions or florid language. However, what is most unique about Lee's literary style is the way in which she uses dialect in characters' dialogue. There are many kinds of dialects that various characters use in *To Kill a Mockingbird.* Atticus Finch speaks in a very formal and educated way. Scout uses informal language and is often reprimanded for this by Aunt Alexandra.

Toward the beginning of the book, Scout and Dill are talking about Dill's father, when Scout catches Dill in a lie about his father's beard. Scout knows that Dill doesn't have a father in his life, and says, "Uh huh, caughtcha . . . You said 'fore you were off the train good your daddy had a black beard—."[12] This is the dialect that Scout uses, although she begins to speak standard English when she is in the company of adult strangers or trying to impress someone.

Lee's realistic use of dialect extends to all characters in her novels. Children who come from poorer families, such as Walter Cunningham, speak differently than Scout or adults like Atticus Finch and Aunt Alexandra. For example, when Miss Caroline picks on Walter for not bringing food with him to school—Scout defends him to the teacher because she understands that his family is too poor to provide him with lunch—Walter responds to her in a drawl. "Nome thank you ma'am," he tells Miss Caroline when she offers him some change to buy lunch, knowing that he would never be able to pay her back.[13]

Calpurnia, the African American housekeeper who raised Scout and Jem after their mother's death, is a unique character because she is able to transition between different levels of language. Scout recognizes when Calpurnia is speaking formal English, which she speaks without fault as a very educated woman. But with Jem and Scout, as well as with her own family and friends, she speaks in her own dialect. Harper Lee's deft use of Calpurnia's different registers of speaking shows the role Calpurnia feels she must play as a black woman in Maycomb, Alabama, during the 1930s. Because of racism and the Jim Crow laws in the South, Calpurnia occupies a precarious position. She must speak in a certain way to show her education to those who do not know her and who would believe, because of racist assumptions, that she is "ignorant." But with her family and those who do not judge her based on her race, she feels free to speak in the dialect that comes most naturally to her, as dialect also comes naturally to Scout, Jem, and even Walter Cunningham.

Thus, the language that Lee uses in her characters' dialogue helps characterize them. The way in which they speak gives readers vital insight into who they are and where they come from, as well as their fears and hopes.

characterization

A literary device an author uses to construct and present a character to readers, usually through dialogue, physical description, and the characters' interactions with others.

Calpurnia, left, was a mother figure for Jem and Scout. She was portrayed by Estelle Evans in the film.

Characterization

Just as the town of Maycomb comes alive with Harper Lee's masterful writing, so, too, do the characters jump off the page and become real people in the eyes of readers. In fact, readers and critics alike have pointed to Lee's ability to build realistic and sympathetic characters as the cornerstone of the book—and the reason why so many have fallen in love with it.

Atticus Finch

Atticus is a lawyer and state representative who raises his son and daughter, Jem and Scout, after the death of his wife and their mother. Atticus is the hero of the novel, who stands up for what he believes in even though he and his children are threatened because of his decision.

Jean Louise "Scout" Finch

Scout is a feisty tomboy who loves wearing overalls and playing imaginative games with her older brother, Jem, and their friend Dill. The novel takes place during formative years in her life—from when she is six to nine years old—and Scout learns throughout the course of the novel that life isn't as simple as she imagined and that justice must be fought for.

Jeremy "Jem" Finch

Jem is Scout's older brother. He ages from ten years old to thirteen years old during the course of the novel. Jem likes to prove that he is fearless and wants to fit in, which leads him to distance himself from his younger sister as he goes to middle school. However, Jem also has a deep empathy and sense of understanding for those who experience racial or social injustice.

Charles Baker "Dill" Harris

Dill is Jem and Scout's neighborhood friend. He lives with his Aunt Rachel during the summers, who is the Finch's next-door neighbor. Dill's imagination is powerful and plays an important role in his life. He lives in a fantasy world, partly because of his tough life. He is from Mississippi but is shuttled around to different relatives because his mother is unwilling or unable to care for him.

Arthur "Boo" Radley

Boo Radley is Jem, Scout, and Dill's obsession. Rumors circulate about him because he never leaves his house. It is said he once attacked his father with a pair of scissors and was put into a mental institution. However, none of these rumors are true. Boo has extreme social anxiety and, because of this, can't leave the house, but he is a kind and gentle soul.

Alexandra Hancock

Aunt Alexandra is Atticus's sister and Jem and Scout's aunt. She is prim and proper and believes that there is a right way to do things. She and Scout are often at odds with one another. Aunt Alexandra is fiercely loyal to her brother and moves in to help him with the children during the court case.

John "Jack" Finch

Uncle Jack is Atticus's younger brother. He is a doctor and a scholar who lives in Boston. The children love him, especially Scout, because he relates to them not as an adult to a child, but as equals. Uncle Jack plays a larger role in *Go Set a Watchman* than in this novel.

Calpurnia

Calpurnia is the Finch's African American housekeeper. However, she plays a maternal role to the children and has taken care of them since the death of their mother. Calpurnia is very educated and holds the status of an equal in the Finch household, where she is respected by Atticus and the children. However, we find out that not everyone thinks like this—because of her race, other Maycomb townspeople look down on the Finch family for treating Calpurnia as an equal.

Tom Robinson

Tom is a black man who is accused of raping Mayella Ewell, the white daughter of Bob Ewell. He is married and is a father. He is a kind man who takes pity on Mayella and tries to help her when she asks, even though he knows this could be dangerous for him since he is a black man. He has an injured left arm that he cannot use, which proves that he would have been unable to attack Mayella as she and her father claim.

Maudie Atkinson

Miss Maudie is a neighbor of the Finches and one of Scout's favorite adults. She has no pretentions and is kind and generous to the children. She believes that all people should be treated equally no matter their race and stands up for what she believes in. Scout spends a lot of time in her house or yard speaking with Maudie or eating her delicious cakes.

Bob Ewell

Bob Ewell is the father of eight children, including Mayella Ewell. He lives in squalor, doesn't work, and uses his government aid to drink

climax

The climax of a plot is the most intense or important scene in a literary work.

The children (far upper right) watch the trial in the "colored" balcony. Blacks and whites were segregated in the courthouse.

while his children barely have enough money to eat. He beats Mayella for speaking with Tom Robinson and then blames the attack and fabricated rape on Tom. At the end of the novel, he tries to hurt Jem and Scout on the way home from their school pageant in revenge for Atticus's defense of Tom Robinson. He is killed by Boo Radley in self-defense.

Enlightenment and Climax

Perhaps the most poignant moments in *To Kill a Mockingbird* occur during and immediately after Scout, Dill, and Jem sneak into the Maycomb courthouse to watch their father defend Tom Robinson, who is on trial for the rape of Mayella Ewell. The children sit in the "colored" balcony. Scout, who had previously accepted Maycomb's treatment of its black population, begins to realize that bigotry and racism means that people like Tom Robinson are not only treated unfairly, but they are also denied justice and often lose their lives.

During the trial, Dill tells Scout that the way Mr. Gilmer, the prosecuting lawyer, cross-examines Tom makes him sick. "The way that man called him 'boy' all the time and sneered at him, an' looked around at the jury every time he answered—," Dill begins before Scout cuts him off. "Well, Dill," Scout says, "after all he's just a Negro."[14] Scout has internalized the values of segregated Maycomb, while Dill is more angered about Mr. Gilmer's racist treatment of Tom. Outside the courthouse, however, they meet Mr. Dolphus Raymond, a white man who is considered a pariah by Maycomb society because he has married and had children with a black woman. He confides in the children that he pretends to have a drinking problem, although he doesn't. He hides Coca-Cola in a paper sack when he sits out in the street pretending to be drunk. The reason he does this, he explains, is because of people's criticism of him. If

Separate water fountains for blacks and whites were a common sight in the South during the Jim Crow era.

they think he is an alcoholic, it gives him a reason for breaking the racial barriers and having a mixed-race family.

When Scout asks Mr. Raymond why he has confided his deepest secret to them, he answers, "Because you're children and you can understand it."[15] Although Scout has already begun to adopt the values of white society in Maycomb, she is still open enough—and innocent enough—as a child to question what she is seeing. She is not yet set in her ways.

Again and again in *To Kill a Mockingbird*, Lee's characters speak about the innate intelligence and understanding of children. It is because of their innocence of the adult world, in fact, that children often see more clearly than adults. And it is the understanding—and compassion—of children that lends readers hope that our world will get better. Indeed, since the publication of *To Kill a Mockingbird* in 1960, much has changed. Jim Crow was struck down, civil rights activists achieved major victories against institutionalized racism, and, while many people continue to fight a necessary battle for increased civil rights, hearts and minds have changed. Today, *To Kill a Mockingbird*, while still relatable to a contemporary audience, seems a cherished relic of times past—we hope that we are living in a more accepting and tolerant time.

Reviews

To Kill a Mockingbird has many fans. Jon Meacham, a well-known editor and presidential biographer, was impressed by the "moral ambiguity" of the novel's ending. "I think the courageous thing that Miss Lee did was end it on a tragic note. You would think in a novel like this, that's achieved this kind of status, it would be a very melodramatic tale of good and evil. Instead, it's a tale of good and evil that ends on a note of gray, which is where most of us live."[16]

There is never any justice for Tom Robinson, as there wasn't for the thousands of African Americans who lived during Jim Crow. Atticus fought for justice for Tom Robinson and lost. This is the hardest lesson that the Finch children need to learn in order to grow up: Justice does not always prevail as we think it should. Oftentimes, the most real change we can hope for comes within ourselves. Jem and Scout are forever changed as they observe the trial in which Tom Robinson is convicted for a crime he did not commit. Their enlightenment—and, later, Scout's refusal to continue tolerating this discrimination—becomes an act of protest in itself.

But it's not just the characters' actions within *To Kill a Mockingbird* that protest against racial discrimination in the Jim Crow South. Harper Lee's decision to write the book was an act of protest during a time when "separate but equal" was still the accepted system of the day. Following the novel's publication, critics lavished praise on the author and her work, all while underlining the fact that the novel would "come under some fire in the Deep South."[17] In many schools across the country, *To Kill a Mockingbird* was banned because of its language, content, and even the fact that it challenged racial discrimination. Pulitzer Prize–winning historian Diane McWhorter, who wrote *Carry Me Home: Birmingham, Alabama: The Climactic Battle of the Civil Rights Revolution*, states, "For a white person from the South to write a book like this in the late 1950s is really unusual—by its very existence an act of protest." Andrew Young, a former UN ambassador, politician, and civil rights activist agrees. He says, "It was an act of protest, but it was an act of humanity . . . It was saying that we're not all like this. There are people who rise above their prejudices and even above the law."[18]

REDISCOVERY AND CONTROVERSY

In November 2014, Harper Lee's sister, Alice, passed away at the age of 103. That summer, HarperCollins announced that it would be publishing Lee's second novel, which had been discovered by Tonja Carter, Harper's lawyer—and Alice Lee's protégé—in the author's safe deposit box.

For many people, this seemed like too much of a coincidence. Why was the book announced so shortly after Alice Lee's death, especially if Harper's sister spent her life protecting her famous sibling from exploitation? Some journalists have stated that, after her stroke, Harper was deaf, nearly blind, and restricted to a wheelchair. In bringing up her health, they questioned whether or not she was mentally capable to give permission to HarperCollins to publish *Go Set a Watchman*—especially if, as some have suggested, Harper signed the contract only weeks after her sister's death.

From 2007 until her death, Harper Lee lived in a nursing home in Monroeville. Her friend, the pastor and historian Wayne Flynt, insisted that Lee was as mentally sharp as ever. In response to the announcement of her second book, he said:

> We have perfectly lucid, rational and detailed conversations . . . I cannot tell you what she and Tonja Carter did and did not discuss about this new book. But this narrative that Nelle Lee does not have the ability to make her mind up about important decisions is just not correct . . . Perhaps [the reason why she decided to

publish her first book in fifty years is because] she has all the privacy she needs now . . . She's in a nursing home in a place where the world can't reach her. Perhaps she feels safe and protected there. But only she and Tonja Carter can know that. For the rest of us, it's just speculation. [1]

Other friends of Harper's, however, mentioned that they were surprised at the announcement and wondered whether Harper was influenced in some way. Marja Mills, a neighbor of Harper and Alice Lee, who wrote a biography about the sisters, says that Alice was concerned about her sister getting exploited for good reason. Alice Lee wrote her a letter in 2011 claiming that her sister "can't see and can't hear and will sign anything put before her by anyone in whom she has confidence." [2]

In fact, the publisher of *Go Set a Watchman* has stated that no one ever spoke directly with Harper Lee and that they only communicated the deal through Tonja Carter and Harper's literary agent. Lee released a statement saying that she was "happy as hell" that the book would be released for readers. [3]

Some people have pointed out that there is evidence that Lee was exploited for the financial interests of those who worked with her. In 2013, Lee, with the aid of her sister, sued a literary agent, claiming that he had tricked her into signing over to him the copyright of *To Kill a Mockingbird*. The lawsuit stated that, soon after she suffered a stroke in 2007, the son of her longtime agent tricked her into signing over her rights to the novel. Lee has stated that she has no recollection of this. This is not the only lawsuit Lee has ever brought to court. She has stated that one of the reasons why she decided to stay out of the limelight—and to stop writing books for publication—

was because she grew angry and frustrated over those people who tried to exploit her for their own financial gain.

The state of Alabama, after hearing complaints from some of Lee's friends and relatives, decided to do its own investigation into the contract that would allow the publication of *Go Set a Watchman*. State investigators interviewed Harper, aides at the nursing home where she resides, and her friends and family. They stated that it was a potential case of "elder abuse," because of Lee's declining health.

Alabama's investigation into claims of elder abuse against Lee did not prove that she was coerced into a new publishing contract. The investigation concluded that Lee signed the contract of her own free will.

> **biography**
>
> The details of a typically famous person's life, written by someone else.

But critics continue to deride HarperCollins's decision to publish the novel—as well as Tonja Carter's "rediscovery" of the manuscript. Whether or not Lee was coerced into the publication of the novel is irrelevant, say some critics, such as Joe Nocera of the *New York Times*. He calls the publication of *Go Set a Watchman* "one of the epic money grabs in the modern history of American publishing."[4] Nocera states that whether or not Harper wanted the book published, the publishing house's marketing of the book was immoral. They knew right away that the manuscript was an earlier draft of Harper Lee's famous novel, but chose to market it as a new novel to create buzz and, eventually, to sell more copies.

Nocera accuses Tonja Carter of having found the manuscript in 2011 and not in 2014, based on reporting done by the *Times*. He states:

The *Times's* account suggests an alternate scenario: that Carter had been sitting on the discovery of the manuscript since 2011, waiting for the moment when she, not Alice, would be in charge of Harper Lee's affairs.

That's issue No. 1. Issue No. 2 is the question of whether "Go Set a Watchman" is, in fact, a "newly discovered" novel, worthy of the hoopla it has received, or whether it is something less than that: a historical artifact or, more bluntly, a not-very-good first draft that eventually became, with a lot of hard work and smart editing, an American classic.

The Murdoch empire is insisting on the former, of course; that's what you do when you're hoping to sell millions of books in an effort to boost the bottom line.[5]

Tonja Carter, however, remembers these events differently. She states, "[A]t some earlier time, I had seen mention of a character who did not make it through the final edit of *Mockingbird* . . . I decided to check to see if maybe that character was in a second book. That is when I went back to the safe deposit box for a more careful look and discovered *Go Set a Watchman*."[6]

Whatever the case, after Alabama's investigation found no wrongdoing on the part of Lee's lawyer or publisher, the issue was dropped. Many people have questioned the morality of marketing the book, which was originally a draft of a previous novel, as a "new novel." But this is a separate issue.

According to Lee's close friends, she was surprised when Tonja Carter told her that she had found the manuscript. Initially, she hadn't wanted to publish it. It had taken some convincing. Joy Williams Brown, Lee's close friend who, along with her husband, originally gave her the gift to work on *To*

Upon the news that *Go Set a Watchman* would be published in 2015, some people questioned whether Lee was mentally and physically capable of approving the book's release.

Kill a Mockingbird for a year, said that she sent it out to friends first and asked their opinions. When everyone said that it was an extraordinary book, she decided to publish it. Her stipulation: that the book be published as is, without any further editing. Only light copyediting was done to the original manuscript, according to the publisher.

If nothing else, the novel is a fascinating look at the work of an author. A few passages remain completely intact from *Go Set a Watchman* in *To Kill a Mockingbird*, proof that the recently published novel was indeed a first draft of Lee's classic. The setting remains largely the same, as both take place in fictitious Maycomb, Alabama. But the time in which the novel is set differs over twenty years. *To Kill a Mockingbird* is set in the 1930s during the Great Depression. This is a period where the social fabric of the United States is nearly torn apart because of increasing poverty. References are made to the rise of Hitler in Germany, which would soon lead to World War II.

Scout's world in *Go Set a Watchman* is very different. There is another crisis at home, which is the battle to end the Jim Crow laws—the battle for civil rights. Scout experiences this as an adult, which infuses her with a sense of responsibility and even anger that she cannot know or experience as a young child.

While many of the characters are similar, several important characters in *To Kill a Mockingbird* do not appear at all in its first draft. Jem appears in Scout's memories in *Go Set a Watchman* but not in the present action. Shockingly, readers find out early in this novel that Jem passed away several years before the current action of the plot. Part of the voyage that Scout must take while reencountering her hometown is a voyage of grief over her brother's death. Dill, too, shows up

Despite the controversy surrounding its publication, copies of *Go Set a Watchman* flew off bookstore shelves.

often in Scout's memories but remains absent in the present plot. There is some anticipation that Dill will reenter—anticipation that Scout feeds, herself, in her desire for him to come back into her life—but he never materializes. Dill spent time fighting in World War II and never returned; instead, he is living like a "free spirit" and traveling around Europe. Like Scout, readers can assume that Dill feels stifled by his past in Maycomb. But no resolution ever appears between these characters.

Atticus Finch's first incarnation in *Go Set a Watchman* is more complex than how he is described in *To Kill a Mockingbird*. No longer a vaunted hero, Atticus is a successful man who has let his success blind him to the plight of others. The complexity of his character is that he attempts to do good, yet remains blind to how his paternalism—and his stone-cold rationality—does real damage to those fighting for their rights.

Lee had to essentially rewrite her first novel to turn it into the classic that it would become. She turned Scout into a child narrator, expanded the characters of Dill and Jem, and took out the complex ethical questioning that pits Atticus and his daughter against one another. Rather than set the novel during the civil rights era, Lee set it during a time when racial and social tension simmered just below the surface. It was a way of making the novel more palatable to a wider audience. This took extensive revisions.

An investigator for the state of Alabama, Joseph Borg, explained why he did not find Lee's associates guilty of "elder abuse." He said, "We're not medically trained. We don't do mental capacity tests. But she knew she was publishing a book. I don't remember her exact words, but they were something like, 'Why the hell would I write a book and not want it published?'" A later statement by Lee released by HarperCollins stated, "I'm alive and kicking and happy as hell with the reactions to *Watchman*."[7]

While it might be easier to state without reservation that HarperCollins's motivation to publish *Go Set a Watchman* was based on a potential financial windfall and the press that would go along with it, it is harder to say whether or not it goes directly against Harper Lee's wishes. Whatever the case, Lee seemed to have no qualms about stating her opinions. The woman who once responded to a journalist's fawning request for an interview by scrawling, "Go away—Harper Lee," has not lost any of her fire—or her sense of humor.

GO SET A WATCHMAN

In *Go Set a Watchman*, Scout returns home to Maycomb after years of living in New York City. She is now an independent adult. Her view of Maycomb is much different than it was when she was younger. In fact, she states many times that she cannot return to live in her hometown. People are too closed, she says, and too "Southern." Scout takes the train from New York back home to visit her father, now elderly. She recounts what she sees as she arrives back home:

> The countryside and the train had subsided to a gentle roll, and she could see nothing but pastureland and black cows from window to horizon. She wondered why she had never thought her country beautiful . . .

> Home was Maycomb County, a gerrymander some seventy miles long and spreading thirty miles at its widest point, a wilderness dotted with tiny settlements the largest of which was Maycomb, the county seat. Until comparatively recently in its history, Maycomb County was so cut off from the rest of the nation that some of its citizens, unaware of the South's political predilections over the past ninety years, still voted Republican. No trains went there . . .the Federal Government had forced a highway or two through the swamps . . . But few people took advantage of the roads, and why should they? If you did not want much, there was plenty. [1]

Returning home, Scout cannot ignore the beauty of her county. But as an adult, she understands how isolated her hometown is. She sees it through a different lens now that she has lived in New York City for many years and experienced a different life. And, yet, it still holds power over her. The evocative imagery Lee uses to describe Maycomb shows both the attachment Scout feels to her town, as well as the power that the setting holds over her characters.

Setting and Background

Lee's second novel is set—and was written—during the mid-1950s at the beginning of the civil rights movement in the United States. In 1954, a historic Supreme Court case, called *Brown vs. Board of Education of Topeka,* ruled that segregated and separate public schools for black students and white students were unconstitutional. After this, some states and cities began a program of integration to place students, both

THE MONTGOMERY BUS BOYCOTT

On December 1, 1955, Rosa Parks, a black woman, refused to give up her seat to a white passenger in Montgomery, Alabama. This was the beginning of the Montgomery bus boycott, which would last until 1956. For over one year, African American residents of Montgomery refused to take public buses until they received the same treatment as white passengers. Reverend Dr. Martin Luther King Jr. helped organize the activists and actively worked on their campaign.

In 1956, a Supreme Court ruling, *Browder v. Gayle,* declared the segregation of public buses unconstitutional. This was a seminal event in the civil rights movement and one of its earliest victories.

African Americans walked to work rather than take the bus during the Montgomery bus boycott of 1955–1956.

black and white, together in the same schools. However, many states resisted this Supreme Court decision. Southern states such as Alabama refused to integrate their schools and faced pressure from the federal government. Some states preferred to close down schools rather than to integrate them.

These early moments were just a starting point in the long battle for racial justice and equality during the civil rights movement. Alabama was a state whose government was one of the most resistant to change. When Scout returns to Maycomb on vacation after living in New York for years, she takes with her everything she hears in the streets of New York and in the New York newspapers about what is occurring in her home state. She knows that groups called "citizens' councils" are smaller, town-based groups of larger white supremacist networks throughout the southern United States. The goal of most of these citizens' councils is to stop the desegregation of schools and to keep white residents and black residents separated. That's why Scout is horrified when, early in her trip, she discovers that her father and her boyfriend, Hank, are active members of a Maycomb citizens' council. In fact, Atticus sits on its board of directors. She discovers this when she finds a pamphlet, entitled *The Black Plague,* at her father's house and asks her Aunt Alexandra about it. Scout says:

> It had something to do with that pamphlet she found in the house—sitting there before God and everybody—something to do with citizens' councils. She knew about them, all right. New York papers [were] full of it. She wished she had paid more attention to them, but only one glance down a column of print was enough to tell her a familiar story: same people who were the Invisible Empire, who hated Catholics; ignorant, fear-ridden, red-faced, boorish, law-abiding, one hundred per cent

red-blooded Anglo-Saxons, her fellow Americans— trash.[2]

Although Scout says that she doesn't keep up with the news, she has a definite feeling that the people involved in the white supremacist groups, including citizens' councils, are close-minded people who have fought against groups of people, including Catholics, Jews, immigrants, and African Americans. In fact, Scout understands that white supremacists fight against anyone who is not exactly like them. She is furious—and fearful—that the person she loves most in the world, her father, would be associated with them.

Conflict

This internal conflict within Scout—before she confronts her father—provides tension for the rest of the book. Only when she confronts Atticus are her fears confirmed. Atticus is active in the citizens' council, he explains, because he dislikes how northern states—and the federal government—are dictating how southern states must govern. As a lawyer who knows the Constitution and believes strongly in a traditional reading of this important document, Atticus feels that states must keep their rights over what occurs in their own borders, without being forced to do things by order of the federal government.

But that's not all. Atticus asks his daughter, "Jean Louise . . . Have you ever considered that you can't have a set of backward people living among people advanced in one kind of civilization and have a social Arcadia?"[3] Atticus means that because African Americans have been treated unfairly for many years and restricted in politics and education, they should not be granted full political and educational opportunities but should be eased into full citizenship. This is an old argument that was used for many years to restrict the freedoms of African Americans in the United States.

Atticus continues: "[S]o far in my experience, white is white and black's black. So far, I've not heard an argument that has convinced me otherwise . . . Now think about this. What would happen if all the Negroes in the South were suddenly given full civil rights? I'll tell you. There'd be another Reconstruction. Would you want your state governments run by people who don't know how to run 'em?"[4]

Scout is shocked by Atticus's words. They are the words that many racists throughout history have used in order to prevent equal rights for African Americans in the United States. Atticus acknowledges that black citizens deserve protection under the law, but he still treats them as "backward" children who cannot—and must not—have the same opportunities as him because of their economic, political, and social disenfranchisement.

Suddenly, Scout realizes the privilege Atticus has had his whole life that has enabled him to create divisions between himself and other people. Atticus worked hard to become a lawyer and put his brother through medical school, but he came from a well-known family in Maycomb, and he had the opportunity to create a nice life for himself. He had the opportunity to choose how he wanted to live. He cannot understand that other people do not have those opportunities because of racial inequality.

> **conflict**
>
> The conflict is what provides tension in a literary work and is a struggle between two opposing forces. Typically, literary characters can experience internal conflicts, which occur within their own mind, or external conflicts, which occur with other characters or within their environment.

This is shocking for a modern-day audience as well as for readers who loved the character of Atticus Finch in *To Kill a Mockingbird* and held him up as a model for racial justice. Critics have mentioned, however, that Atticus always showed these characteristics even in Lee's first novel.

Katie Rose Guest Pryal, a novelist and former law professor, analyzes the character of Atticus Finch from a legal perspective. During the court case against Tom Robinson, she says, there is no effort on the part of Atticus to understand the background or personality of the man he is defending. She calls this a "failure of empathy" on the part of Atticus in *To Kill a Mockingbird* and states, "Neither the jury nor the audience of the novel have learned anything about Tom: where he lives,

Members of the Alabama Citizens' Council meet to discuss segregation. In *Go Set a Watchman*, Scout is devastated when she realizes her father is a member of such a citizens' council.

what his family is like, how he treats his wife and children and others in his daily life."[5]

Another legal scholar, Professor Ann Engar, states, "In the imagination he is much greater than he is in the actual books . . . In [*To Kill a Mockingbird*], for example, Atticus Finch is assigned to defend Tom Robinson. He doesn't volunteer to do it.[6]

Thus, the unjust court case that should be about Tom Robinson in order to prove his innocence becomes about saving Atticus's own honor. Even Jem, Scout, and Dill, who watch the court case from the "colored balcony," spend much of the court case impressed by Atticus's legal efforts. Some critics and activists have decried the secondary role that Tom plays to Atticus's legal prowess. To them, the plot of *Go Set a Watchman* bears out their critiques—Atticus is not a hero, but rather a man who spends a lot of time protecting his honor, his family name, and what he imagines to be "the way things are and must be." Atticus, thus, is not the transformative figure that we imagine him to be. In Lee's second novel, he is a stalwart who refuses to change—once again, it is his fear of losing status that leads him to join the infamous citizens' council.

Plot

Jean Louise "Scout" Finch returns home to Maycomb, Alabama, to visit her aging father, Atticus, two years after the sudden death of her brother, Jem, caused by the genetic heart condition that killed their mother many years ago. Now in her mid-twenties, Jean Louise lives in New York City and comes back home only once a year. Her boyfriend, Henry "Hank" Clifton, is a rising-star lawyer under the tutelage of Atticus and was a childhood friend of Jean Louise. Jean Louise, however, feels very conflicted about her relationship with him. On the

Brock Peters portrays Tom Robinson as he takes the stand in his rape trial. Symbolically, Tom is one of Lee's mockingbirds; he is a good, innocent man who is wrongly accused.

one hand, she knows that she can never marry him because she cannot move back to Maycomb and does not want to be a typical Maycomb wife and mother. On the other hand, the two share a past and a deep connection, and Jean Louise imagines that she will never find anyone else with whom to share her life.

While at home, Jean Louise sees a pamphlet in her father's study. It is a racist pamphlet and, at first, she cannot believe that her father would actually have such a hateful document in his home. Aunt Alexandra, however, tells Jean Louise that both her father and Hank sit on the Maycomb citizens' council, which is how he got the pamphlet. Jean Louise follows them to the Maycomb courthouse, where the council meets, and sees their involvement for herself. She is shocked and dismayed.

Later, the tension between Jean Louise and her father grows. Calpurnia's grandson kills a pedestrian while driving and Atticus agrees to defend him. However, he states that he will defend Calpurnia's grandson not necessarily just to prove his innocence, but because he doesn't want the NAACP coming to Maycomb to take over his defense. After Jean Louise goes to Calpurnia's house to offer support, she realizes the depth of the racial tension in her hometown. Calpurnia, who was once like a mother to Jean Louise, won't even look at her.

Jean Louise's own anger boils over when she speaks with Hank and confronts him about his joining the citizens' council. She tells him she would never be able to marry him. Hank tells her that she, unlike him, is privileged enough to have the option to stand up for her beliefs. When Jean Louise turns around, she sees that her father is standing behind her, listening to their conversation.

In *Go Set a Watchman*, Atticus does not want the NAACP to interfere in events in town. The civil rights group assisted those whom they believed had been unjustly accused. Here, Rosa Parks arrives at her trial with president of the NAACP, E.D. Nixon.

Jean Louise confronts her father in his office. Atticus states that he believes that all men and women are created equal, but he doesn't like civil rights legislation being forced onto the states by the federal government. He also states his belief that African American men and women are not ready to become full citizens of the United States following many years of discrimination and oppression. This infuriates Scout and she runs back home to pack and leave Maycomb for good.

In her fury, Jean Louise is approached by Uncle Jack, who slaps her across the face. He tells her that Atticus was waiting for her to confront him and to understand that they are different people with different moralities. It is time, he says, for her to accept that Atticus is only human. This is a shock to Jean Louise, but she gradually begins to understand. At the end of the novel, she speaks with her father, who tells her he is happy that she has formed her own opinions that diverge from his own. She tells him that she loves him and "silently welcome[s] him to the human race."[7]

Characterization

Many of the beloved characters from *To Kill a Mockingbird* reappear in *Go Set a Watchman*, including Scout (now referred to mostly by her real name, Jean Louise), Atticus, Aunt Alexandra, Uncle Jack, and Calpurnia. However, these characters have changed and, in some ways, share little with the characters of Lee's first novel. Jem appears only in flashbacks, as readers learn that he passed away before the current action of the novel. Jean Louise often speaks of and thinks about Dill, who is living in Europe, but he never returns to Maycomb during the course of the novel.

Atticus Finch

Atticus Finch has aged, his daughter is surprised to note when she returns home to visit him. Jem's death greatly affected him, and his hair is starting to turn gray at seventy-two. He is still active in local politics and is a successful lawyer who takes Henry "Hank" Clinton under his tutelage after the death of his son. Atticus is very different in some ways from the character readers came to know in *To Kill a Mockingbird*: He is against the racial integration of schools, the actions of the NAACP, and the federal government's mandate to end Jim Crow laws in the southern United States.

Jean Louise Finch

Jean Louise Finch—who is no longer called by her nickname, "Scout," except by her immediate family—has grown up to become a young woman who is passionate for justice. Her hometown of Maycomb can no longer contain her. She lives in New York and feels that she can never again be restricted by the closed minds of her hometown. She doesn't fit in at home in other ways as well—Jean Louise has no immediate desire to get married or have children like most of her contemporaries back home, although she does feel the pressure to bend to these societal norms.

Alexandra Finch

Aunt Alexandra is still a prim and proper southern woman who wants her niece, Jean Louise, to act according to her social status. Jean Louise states unequivocally upon returning home that she and Aunt Alexandra have never gotten along—and that she would never understand her aunt. However, Alexandra does prove to have a good heart for her family. After Jem's unexpected death, she moves in with Atticus to take care of him. Furthermore, after Jean Louise confronts Alexandra as she angrily packs her bags, she makes her cry. Jean Louise apologizes and states that she was never "much of a lady" like her aunt. Aunt Alexandra replies, "You're mistaken, Jean Louise, if you think you're no lady."[8] This is the most tender moment Jean Louise shares with her aunt.

John "Jack" Hale Finch

Jean Louise looks up to Uncle Jack and opens up to him about her despair over seeing her father involved in the Maycomb citizens' council. He is an intelligent man who gives advice in literary quotes that other people, less educated in literary matters, have difficulty following. He is also honest, and Jean Louise trusts him more than anyone else. His conversation with Jean Louise toward the end of the novel is revelatory. It is in this conversation that Scout understands the importance of her rebellion against her father—even as she understands the racist ideology that underpins both Atticus and Uncle Jack's beliefs.

Calpurnia

Calpurnia is not seen often in *Go Set a Watchman*, except in one of its most painful scenes. Since Jem's death, which greatly affected her, Calpurnia has retired from working for the Finches and now lives with her children and grandchildren. During the course of the novel, Calpurnia's grandson, Frank, accidentally runs over and kills a white man. Atticus decides to take on the case in order to stop the NAACP from getting involved and says that the best thing that can happen is if Frank pleads guilty. Ashamed and angry at her father's racism, and hoping to comfort her beloved Calpurnia, Jean Louise decides to go visit her. Calpurnia is almost blind and is very feeble, which shocks Jean Louise. But most shocking to Jean Louise is not just Calpurnia's physical changes, but her change in behavior. Calpurnia speaks formally to Jean Louise, calling her "ma'am," and remains distant from the girl she raised.

Henry "Hank" Clinton

Hank is a hardworking lawyer, a veteran of World War II, a close childhood friend to Jean Louise, and her current boyfriend. He is in love with Jean Louise and asks her multiple times to marry him, but Jean Louise refuses. Hank was raised by a poor single mother and started working as a young child to support himself and his mother. His hard work has paid off, as it seems likely that he will take over Atticus's position when he retires. Aunt Alexandra does not approve of Jean Louise's relationship with Hank because of his lower social status—and Hank is acutely aware of his classification as "trash" by Maycomb standards. Hank is not immune to racist assumptions, either, like many of the residents of Maycomb. At the beginning of the novel, Hank comments that African-Americans don't know how to drive, and he is a member of the Maycomb citizens' council with Atticus—although he claims that he felt pressured into joining.

An Important—and Symbolic—Scene

One of the most important scenes in the book occurs when Jean Louise goes to visit Calpurnia after hearing that her grandson was involved in a car accident that killed a white man. Jean Louise is already disillusioned by her father's actions—she has already spied on him at the courthouse during the citizens' council meeting. She wants to speak to Calpurnia and ask if there is anything that she can do to help—this is because of her own guilty conscience over her father's actions.

When Jean Louise sees Calpurnia, her beloved housekeeper acts very strangely. Jean Louise says, "Don't worry, Cal. Atticus'll do his best." To this, Calpurnia responds, "I know he will, Miss Scout. He always do his best. He always do right."[9]

Readers will notice the difference in tone between Jean Louise and Calpurnia's conversation. Jean Louise uses "Cal," an affectionate and informal nickname when addressing Calpurnia. Calpurnia refers to Jean Louise as "Ma'am" and "Miss Scout." This shows the tension between the two figures—Jean Louise has grown up and become a white woman in a society where African Americans do not have the same rights or social status—and where they must defer to their white employers.

Jean Louise recognizes Calpurnia's formality and distance right away:

> Jean Louise stared open-mouthed at the old woman. Calpurnia was sitting in a haughty dignity that appeared on state occasions, and with it appeared erratic grammar. Had the earth stopped turning, had the trees frozen, had the sea given up its dead, Jean Louise would not have noticed . . .

> "Cal," she cried, "Cal, Cal, Cal, what are you doing to me? What's the matter? I'm your baby, have you forgotten me? Why are you shutting me out? What are you doing to me?"

> Calpurnia lifted her hands and brought them down softly on the arms of the rocker. Her face was a million tiny wrinkles, and her eyes were dim behind thick lenses.

> "What are you all doing to us?" she said.[10]

This is an excruciatingly painful moment for Jean Louise, who can't comprehend the resentment that Calpurnia feels and believes she is not personally responsible. But, Calpurnia can no longer pretend that everything is okay. To her, the relationship she has with Jean Louise feeds into the larger problem: The mistreatment of African Americans in the United States, and the refusal of Maycomb's white citizens, including Atticus, to take a stand for racial justice.

This interaction between Jean Louise and Calpurnia symbolizes the larger degradation of relationships between the white residents and black residents of Maycomb and, indeed, the United States. Jean Louise cannot understand how Calpurnia's pain can turn to such anger and she is shocked, but, as a white woman of a high social status, she has never had to deal with such forms of exclusion and discrimination.

At the end of this scene, Jean Louise asks Calpurnia one more question before she leaves:

> "Tell me one thing, Cal," she said, "just one thing before I go—please, I've got to know. Did you hate us?"
>
> The old woman sat silent, bearing the burden of her years. Jean Louise waited.
>
> Finally, Calpurnia shook her head.[11]

Critical Response

While *To Kill a Mockingbird* became an instant sensation upon its publication, even taking its author by surprise, *Go Set a Watchman* has received a wider range of critical responses. Both critics and readers are divided as to the literary merit of the novel, although some critics concede this is because of its publication fifty-five years after it was originally written.

According to Adam Gopnick, writing for the *New Yorker,* *Go Set a Watchman* is a "failure of a novel (if 'Mockingbird' did not exist, this book would never have been published, not now, as it was not then), [though] it is still testimony to how appealing a writer Harper Lee can be."[12] Gopnick concedes the "right" tone of Lee's second novel and its evocative imagery, but states that there are several problems with the novel, including the development of the character of Atticus Finch. If Atticus's character hadn't already been developed so intricately in *To Kill a Mockingbird*, Gopnick argues, readers wouldn't care about the Atticus presented in the second novel, who remains a loose sketch.

> **stand-alone book**
>
> A stand-alone book can be read by itself without knowledge gained from a previous book.

The character of Atticus Finch, as developed in *Go Set a Watchman*, has also caused controversy among other critics. Many readers felt deceived upon hearing Atticus's beliefs about the NAACP's work in the South during the civil rights era. Scout's father, who appeared stridently antiracist in *To Kill a Mockingbird,* appears in this novel to harbor racist sympathies. However, as Gopnick explains, this is another reason for the supposed "failure" of the novel—its material is dated. In the 1950s, public intellectuals often held the views of Atticus Finch—that black men and women should have equality, but that it must occur slowly because of their "ignorance" of society and cannot be dictated by the federal government. This evident bigotry is much more shocking to a contemporary audience because such incarnations of racism during the 1950s were viewed as acceptable and even progressive for the time.

In a review of *Watchman* for the *Guardian,* Mark Lawson explains the deception that readers might feel upon being introduced to this "new" Atticus as "painful."[13] But he also states that the complexities of racial and political beliefs of the time lend *Watchman* more intricacy than Harper Lee's first novel. If the novel is a failure as a stand-alone book, its depictions of the political complexities of the southern United States before the civil rights era make it a success.

Daniel D'Addario, in a review for *Time,* agrees with this assessment. He states:

Watchman is both a painful complication of Harper Lee's beloved book and a confirmation that a novel read widely by schoolchildren is more bitter than sweet . . . The success of *Go Set a Watchman* . . . lies both in its depiction of Jean Louise reckoning with her father's beliefs, and in the manner by which it integrates those beliefs into the Atticus we know. Atticus isn't—never was—a blind fighter for what is empirically right. His true heart, expressed in a lengthy debate with Jean Louise, actually squares neatly with the paternalistic attitude Atticus takes toward black people in *To Kill a Mockingbird,* and his occasionally overwrought compassion for his racist white neighbors.[14]

While the character of Atticus Finch in *Go Set a Watchman* is the most contentious point of debate among readers and critics of the novel, many agree that this new depiction of the Finch patriarch adds both to our understanding of *To Kill a Mockingbird* and to the racial and political complexities of the time.

Conclusion Without Resolution

Many scholars have criticized both of Harper Lee's novels for focusing on white experience and relegating African

Go Set a Watchman paints a more complex portrait of Atticus Finch than does *To Kill a Mockingbird*.

American characters to the background. This, indeed, could be true. While Lee's novels deal with the inequities of the Jim Crow South, they filter these experiences through Scout's limited understanding. In *Go Set a Watchman*, as Scout grows up to become the young adult Jean Louise, the experiences that she's gathered living by herself cause her to question her family's beliefs—and their racist underpinnings. But there are no easy answers, nor resolutions. In fact, *Go Set a Watchman* does not offer any solutions. At the end of the novel, Jean Louise kisses her father and tells him that she loves him, all while understanding that she cannot—and must not—accept his racist beliefs.

Perhaps Uncle Jack says it best when he tells his niece, "The South's in its last agonizing birth pain. It's bringing forth something new and I'm not sure I like it, but I won't be here to see it. You will."[15]

Uncle Jack urges Jean Louise to stay in Maycomb and to understand that there are good people in her hometown who will work hard to make the world a better place. He explains to her that racist beliefs are handed down over generations and that the only way they can be stopped is through people like Jean Louise, who don't run away but who turn their beliefs into action—no matter how long it takes or how frustrating it may be. Indeed, the United States has come a long way since Harper Lee wrote about the devastation caused by the Jim Crow laws in the late 1950s. The civil rights movement continued for nearly ten years after Harper Lee's first attempts at telling her story, and its hard-won victories have changed our world for the better. Perhaps the lesson Lee offers to her readers is simple enough: Never, ever stay silent in the face of injustice.

CHRONOLOGY

1926— Nelle Harper Lee is born in Monroeville, Alabama, on April 28.

1930— Truman Persons moves in with his cousins, who live next door to Harper Lee.

1931— The first Scottsboro Boys trial begins.

1944— Lee begins studying at Huntington College in Alabama.

1945— Transfers to the University of Alabama to study law—she leaves four years later without receiving her degree.

1949— Moves to New York and works for an airline while writing at night.

1951— Lee's mother and brother, Edwin, die.

1956— Receives a generous Christmas gift from her friends Michael and Joy Brown—enough money to quit her job and spend the year writing her novel.

1957— Submits her first manuscript, titled *Go Set a Watchman,* to her agent, who suggests she rewrite it.

1959— Travels to Kansas with her friend Truman Capote (Persons) to investigate the story of the Clutter family's murder, which becomes the bestseller *In Cold Blood.*

1960— *To Kill a Mockingbird* is published to great acclaim.

1961— Lee wins the Pulitzer Prize for her novel.

1962— Film adaptation of *To Kill a Mockingbird*, starring Gregory Peck as Atticus Finch, is released.

2006— Lee publishes her first essay in many years in *O Magazine*, entitled "A Letter to Oprah from Harper Lee."

2007— Inducted into the American Academy of Arts and Letters in May. In November, she is presented the

Presidential Medal of Freedom by President George W. Bush. She suffers a stroke and moves back to Monroeville.

2010— President Barack Obama presents Harper Lee with the National Medal of Arts.

2014— Lee's sister, Alice, passes away.

2015— *Go Set a Watchman* is published by HarperCollins on July 14.

2016— Harper Lee dies on February 19 in Monroeville, Alabama, at the age of eighty-nine.

CHAPTER NOTES

Chapter 1. An Enigmatic Figure

1. Harper Lee, "Christmas to Me," *McCall's*, 1961, http://heyboobooks.tumblr.com/post/2447111228/christmas-to-me-an-essay-by-harper-lee.
2. Harper Lee, "When Children Discover America," *McCall's*, August 1965, http://web.archive.org/web/20070429071626/www.chebucto.ns.ca/culture/HarperLee/when.html.
3. Ibid.
4. William Wordsworth, "Ode: Intimations of Immortality from Recollections of Early Childhood," http://www.bartleby.com/101/536.html.

Chapter 2. A Private Life

1. Jonathan Mahler, "The Invisible Hand Behind Harper Lee's *To Kill a Mockingbird*," *New York Times,* July 12, 2015, http://www.nytimes.com/2015/07/13/books/the-invisible-hand-behind-harper-lees-to-kill-a-mockingbird.html?_r=0.
2. Charles J. Shields, *Mockingbird: A Portrait of Harper Lee* (New York: Henry Holt and Co., 2007), p. 121.
3. Mahler.
4. Ibid.
5. Philip Sherwell, "Harper and Alice Lee, a Story of Two Sisters," *Telegraph*, February 7, 2015, http://www.telegraph.co.uk/news/worldnews/northamerica/usa/11398342/Harper-and-Alice-Lee-a-story-of-two-sisters.html.

Chapter 3. A History of Racial and Social Inequity

1. Harper Lee, *To Kill a Mockingbird* (New York: HarperPerennial, 2002), pp. 5–6.

2. Cary Nelson, "About the Great Depression," The Department of English: Illinois State University, http://www.english.illinois.edu/maps/depression/about.htm.

3. Lee, *To Kill a Mockingbird*, p. 23.

Chapter 4. Innocence Lost and Found: Major Themes

1. Roy Newquist, "Roy Newquist Interviews Harper Lee." Originally from *Counterpoint* (1964), http://web.archive.org/web/20070630230531/www.chebucto.ns.ca/culture/HarperLee/roy.html.

2. Harper Lee, *To Kill a Mockingbird* (New York: HarperPerennial, 2002), pp. 3–4.

3. Ibid., p. 175.

4. Ibid., p. 226.

5. Ibid., p. 265.

6. Ibid., p. 267.

7. Ibid., p. 270.

8. Ibid., p. 234.

9. Ibid., p. 108.

10. Ibid., p. 45.

11. Ibid., p. 14.

12. Ibid., p. 319.

13. Greg Garrison, "*Go Set a Watchman:* What Does Harper Lee's Book Title Mean?" *Al.com,* http://www.al.com/living/index.ssf/2015/02/go_set_a_watchman_whats_the_bi.html.

14. Ibid.

15. Harper Lee, *Go Set a Watchman* (New York: Harper, 2015), p. 264.

16. Ibid., p. 270.

Chapter 5. *To Kill a Mockingbird*

1. Mary Murphy, "Excerpt from Director Mary Murphy's *Scout, Atticus, and Boo.*" *PBS: American Masters,* March 20, 2012, http://www.pbs.org/wnet/americanmasters/harper-lee-hey-boo-excerpt-from-director-mary-murphys-scout-atticus-and-boo/2015/.
2. Ibid.
3. Ibid.
4. Harper Lee, *To Kill a Mockingbird* (New York: HarperPerennial, 2002), p. 1.
5. Murphy.
6. Ibid.
7. Lee, *To Kill a Mockingbird,* p. 103.
8. Ibid., p. 103.
9. Ibid., p. 112.
10. Ibid.
11. Ibid.
12. Harper Lee, *To Kill a Mockingbird* (New York: Grand Central Publishing, 1988), p. 63.
13. Ibid., p. 23.
14. Ibid., p. 226.
15. Ibid., p. 228.
16. Murphy.
17. Joshua Barajas, "How Newspapers Reviewed 'To Kill a Mockingbird' in 1960," *PBS NewsHour,* July 13, 2015, http://www.pbs.org/newshour/art/newspaper-reviews-thought-kill-mockingbird-became-masterpiece/.
18. Murphy.

Chapter 6. Rediscovery and Controversy

1. Philip Sherwell, "Harper and Alice Lee, a Story of Two Sisters," *Telegraph,* February 7, 2015, http://www.telegraph.

co.uk/news/worldnews/northamerica/usa/11398342/
Harper-and-Alice-Lee-a-story-of-two-sisters.html.

2. Alexandra Alter, "Harper Lee, Author of 'To Kill a Mockingbird,' Is to Publish a New Novel," *New York Times*, February 2, 2015, http://www.nytimes.com/2015/02/04/ books/harper-lee-author-of-to-kill-a-mockingbird-is-to-publish-a-new-novel.html?_r=1.

3. Philip Sherwell, "Harper Lee Insists She Is Alive and Kicking and Happy as Hell in Quote Issued by Publisher," *Telegraph*, February 5, 2015, http://www.telegraph. co.uk/news/worldnews/northamerica/usa/11393271/ Harper-Lee-insists-she-is-alive-and-kicking-and-happy-as-hell-in-quote-issued-by-publisher.html.

4. Joe Nocera, "The Harper Lee *Go Set a Watchman* Fraud," *New York Times,* July 14, 2015, http://www.nytimes. com/2015/07/25/opinion/joe-nocera-the-watchman-fraud.html?_r=0.

5. Ibid.

6. Claire Suddath, "What Does Harper Lee Want?" *Bloomberg Business,* July 19, 2015, http://www.bloomberg.com/ graphics/2015-harper-lee-go-set-a-watchman/.

7. Ibid.

Chapter 7. *Go Set a Watchman*

1. Harper Lee, *Go Set a Watchman* (New York: Harper, 2015), p. 9.

2. Ibid., p. 104.

3. Ibid., p. 242.

4. Ibid., p. 246.

5. Lisa Marsh, "These Scholars Have Been Pointing Out Atticus Finch's Racism for Years," *New Republic,* July 14, 2015, http://newrepublic.com/article/122295/these-scholars-have-been-pointing-out-atticus-finchs-racism-years.

6. Ibid.

7. Lee, *Go Set a Watchman*, p. 278.

8. Ibid., p. 259.

9. Ibid., p. 159.

10. Ibid., pp. 159–160.

11. Ibid., p. 160.

12. Adam Gopnick, "Sweet Home Alabama: Harper Lee's Go Set a Watchman," *The New Yorker,* July 27, 2015, http://www.newyorker.com/magazine/2015/07/27/sweet-home-alabama.

13. Mark Lawson, "*Go Set a Watchman* Review—More Complex than Harper Lee's Original Classic, But Less Compelling," *The Guardian,* July 13, 2015, http://www.theguardian.com/books/2015/jul/12/go-set-a-watchman-review-harper-lee-to-kill-a-mockingbird.

14. Daniel D'Addario, "*Go Set a Watchman* Review: Atticus Finch's Racism Makes Scout, and Us, Grow Up," *Time,* July 11, 2015, http://time.com/3954581/go-set-a-watchman-review/.

15. Lee, *Go Set a Watchman*, p. 142.

Literary Terms

anecdotes—Short or interesting stories used for entertainment or instruction.

biography—The details of a typically famous person's life, written by someone else.

characterization—A literary device an author uses to construct and present a character to readers, usually through dialogue, physical description, and the characters' interactions with others.

climax—The climax of a plot is the most intense or important scene in a literary work.

conflict—The conflict is what provides tension in a literary work and is a struggle between two opposing forces. Typically, literary characters can experience internal conflicts, which occur within their own mind, or external conflicts, which occur with other characters or within their environment.

dialect—A particular form of language that is used by a specific group of people who share a common background, social status, or geographic location.

first-person narration—When one person narrates the story using the first person.

imagery—The author's use of vivid language and description to paint a visual picture for his or her readers.

metaphor—A literary device used to compare something to an unrelated thing for literary effect.

narrative structure—The way in which the content of a story is organized and presented to the reader.

plot twist—An unexpected event that changes the course of the plot.

provenance—The beginning of something.

resolution—The moment in the plot of a story when a problem is solved or come to terms with.

satire—A form of humor used to make fun of perceived stupidity, especially used to critique politics or social issues.

sensory details—Writing that engages at least one of the reader's five senses: sight, sound, taste, touch, and smell.

stand-alone book—A stand-alone book can be read by itself without knowledge gained from a previous book.

symbolism—The use of symbols, or a thing that represents something else, to convey a theme or ideas.

WORKS BY
HARPER LEE

Novels

To Kill a Mockingbird
Go Set a Watchman

Essays

"Love—In Other Words" (1961)
"Christmas to Me" (1961)
"When Children Discover America" (1965)
"Romance and High Adventure" (1983)
"Open Letter to Oprah Winfrey" (2006)

Further Reading

Capote, Truman. *In Cold Blood.* New York: Vintage, 1994.

Kinshasa, Kwando M. *The Scottsboro Boys in Their Own Words: Selected Letters, 1931–1950.* Jefferson, NC: McFarland, 2014.

Mills, Marja. *The Mockingbird Next Door: Life With Harper Lee.* New York: Penguin, 2014.

Shields, Charles J. *I Am Scout: The Biography of Harper Lee.* New York: Henry Holt and Co., 2008.

Williams, Donnie, and Wayne Greenshaw. *The Thunder of Angels: The Montgomery Bus Boycott and the People Who Broke the Back of Jim Crow.* Chicago: Chicago Review Press, 2005.

WEBSITES

Letters of Note: Some Things Should Happen on Soft Pages, Not Cold Metal

www.lettersofnote.com/2012/10/some-things-should-happen-on-soft-pages.html

Read the full text of Lee's letter to Oprah about developing an early love of books.

Monroe County Museum

www.monroecountymuseum.org

The official website of the Old Courthouse Museum presents information on the setting of the Tom Robinson trial and highlights from the Harper Lee exhibit. A section of the website is also dedicated to Truman Capote and his works.

The Big Read: *To Kill a Mockingbird*

www.neabigread.org/books/mockingbird

This site offers biographical information about Harper Lee, as well as a reader's and teacher's guide for her beloved classic.

INDEX